Promoting Rock Concerts

Zadoc Music Business Series

available

Promoting Rock Concerts
    by Howard Stein with Ronald Zalkind
Getting Ahead in the Music Business
    by Ronald Zalkind

in preparation

Producing Hit Records
Understanding Music Business Contracts, 2 vols.
Financial Planning for Entrepreneurs in the Arts
Writing Hit Songs
The Contemporary Music Almanac

Promoting Rock Concerts

by
Howard Stein
with
Ronald Zalkind

A ZADOC BOOK

SCHIRMER BOOKS
A Division of Macmillan Publishing Company, Inc.
NEW YORK

Collier Macmillan Publishers
LONDON

Special thanks to Marian Smith for transcribing tapes, copy editing, and asking good questions; also Terry Holmes for information on load-ins and load-outs.

ZADOC® is a registered trademark protected by law.

Schirmer Books
A Division of Macmillan Publishing Co., Inc.
866 Third Avenue, New York, N.Y. 10022

Collier Macmillan Canada, Ltd.

Library of Congress Catalog Card Number: 79–63032

Printed in the United States of America

printing number
1   2   3   4   5   6   7   8   9   10

Library of Congress Cataloging in Publication Data

Stein, Howard.
   Promoting rock concerts.

   1. Concert agents—Vocational guidance.   I. Zalkind,
Ronald, joint author.   II.   Title.
ML3795.S82   338.4'7'784   79-63032
ISBN 0-02-872470-4

for Martha

Contents

Introduction

POTENTIAL CONCERT PROMOTERS have some very glamorized, unrealistic ideas about this business. Few laymen realize how perilous it is to promote concerts, or the extreme mortality rate that concert promoters suffer.

I've been behind the scenes for more than ten years. I've promoted several thousand concerts, indoors, outdoors, at stadiums, in classical concert halls, in a variety of cities, under almost every conceivable circumstance. What is perhaps most significant, in terms of the utility of this book, is that I've been away from concert promotions for a few years. I can speak about the business objectively. I can, and will, expose some truths about this business that an active promoter, who must maintain good relations with important attractions, managers, and agencies, would be afraid to discuss.

My experience as a promoter/producer (the words are not interchangeable—to promote means to present a self-contained, prepackaged show; to produce means to be able to determine the sound, lights, and content of a show, in concert with the artist, personal manager, and agent, and then to promote the event) is in what I generically call rock and roll. I define rock and roll in terms of its audience: one composed primarily of teenagers, primarily from white middle- and upper-middle-class families. This book, however, transcends the medium of rock. The automatic aspects of promoting a concert, from logistics to advertising to ticket sales, are virtually the same whether you're promoting ballet, rock, classical music, or boxing. My references will be to rock, because that's my real experience. But any person interested in concert promotion as a career will benefit from reading this book.

My purpose is to take a generally confusing and unpredictable business and try to give it as much order and sense as possible. I'll do it by establishing the cast of characters; by examining the facility, or venue; by creating a chronology of how to promote a concert; by analyzing the various costs a concert promoter incurs; by recommending ways to break into the business and develop a career; and much more.

I'll try to strip away the glamorous facade surrounding the business, and offer tangible instructions on how to talk to an agent; how to talk to a manager; how to deliver talent; and how to get that all-important first job.

I'll make it easier to understand agency contracts, riders, and other legal papers binding agents, halls, and promoters together. I'll examine my own production cost analysis worksheets—shorthand reference material that alone may justify your reading this book.

I purposely will avoid mentioning any incidents with which I have been involved, good or bad, with superstar artists, agents, and managers in the business, unless they specifically illustrate the subject at hand. I'm not writing this book for the sake of gossip. I'm writing it to help readers comprehend what it takes to be a successful concert promoter, and whether it makes sense to try concert promotion as a potential career.

I suppose the primary reason I'm no longer promoting rock concerts is that I simply grew out of it. Concert promotion is not the most secure way to make a living, nor does it offer a consistent form of other-than-financial rewards. But for the young in age, and in heart, it will always seem one of the best ways to cement the bond between big bucks and the love of entertainment.

Howard Stein

Promoting
Rock
Concerts

1

Getting to Know Me

I AM BEGINNING this book with a few pages of personal biography so that the reader can understand where I'm coming from. I've promoted more than 2,500 concerts in my career, with acts and facilities that most promoters will only dream about handling. I know the people very well. I know what's exciting about the concert promotion business, and I've been exposed to virtually every conceivable problem a promoter might come across.

My career in the music business began as a concessionaire for my uncle's T-shirt, program, and souvenir merchandising business. It was the early '60s, and the new English groups, like Herman's Hermits and The Animals, were just starting to happen. My uncle, who had trouble relating to rock music, felt that I, a theater student, was the right age and had the right temperament to make personal friends with the people behind this potentially huge new source of business. He invited me to set up and actually hawk his merchandise at the new rock emporiums, or to make arrangements with the local union hawkers to do so. I accepted the job, and started traveling across the United States with major rock groups, sometimes in their chartered planes, sometimes on commercial flights.

In traveling with these groups, I began to gain familiarity with the cast of characters in the concert promotion business. I learned who the heavies were. I learned how the facilities operated. I started brushing shoulders with the various personalities in the industry: agents, managers, hall owners, union representatives. Basically, that's how I learned what the whole thing was about. I was right there: I could see who was hot, who was happening, and how to get results.

Rock and roll at that time was still something of a teenage secret. Part of the valuable expertise I gained, and which I subsequently exploited, was that I knew who sold tickets to this new audience. After working several seasons for my uncle, I went around selling myself as one of the new experts in the rock and roll phenomenon. I was hired as a rock and roll consultant to Music Fair Enterprises, which owned a series of theaters in the round in Westbury, Long Island; Valley Forge, Pennsylvania; and Washington, D.C. My job was to advise Lee Guber and Shelley Gross, the owners of Music Fair Enterprises, which acts would fill their halls on evenings when their major pop attractions, such as Buddy Hackett or Liberace, had the night off.

I was very lucky. I had behind me the power of a nationally known music corporation that operated important facilities. Gradually, my role switched from acting as an advisor to actually buying talent on behalf of Music Fair Enterprises. I then convinced Lee Guber and Shelley Gross to open a summer concert hall, purely for rock and roll, in the New York State Pavilion at the World's Fair site in Flushing Meadow Park. It was called the Pavilion. I was put in charge of the facility, and hired a young staff of people who had worked for Bill Graham at the Fillmore East.

The Pavilion, whose see-through plastic roof provided a natural light show each night, was one of the most beautiful places I've ever worked in. It was a fantastic success for a first-year operation, and became one of the most important rock venues that America has ever had. But the Pavilion never had a second season. Citizen complaints about heavy traffic in the park and the volume of the sound system, coupled with political fights involving Bill Graham, Lee Guber, Shelley Gross, and myself, doomed the Pavilion to a very short run.

By now I had the desire to go out on my own and promote concerts. I couldn't go to New York City, where tacit exclusivities with most major facilities were held by Bill Graham, so I promoted a few spot concerts outside of the city. Shortly thereafter, as a result of the visibility I had achieved working at the Pavilion and as an independent promoter, I was approached by Dee Anthony, who is now Peter Frampton's personal manager, to form a partnership and run the Capitol Theater in Portchester, New York. This was the first suburban rock theater in the United States. Still in my early twenties, I produced all the attractions that Dee Anthony managed at that time, including Joe Cocker, Ten Years After, Traffic, and Jethro Tull.

Dee Anthony's decision to devote more time to personal management and get out of the Capitol Theater coincided with my own plans to form Howard Stein Enterprises. When Bill Graham left the Fillmore East in New York City, I took up residence in Manhattan at the Academy of Music. I raised money on Wall Street by selling myself as a rock and roll genius who had promoted many successful rock concerts at the Pavilion and the Capitol Theater. I survived a disastrous no-show concert involving Aretha Franklin at the Toronto Maple Leaf Garden, my first experience with a major sports arena and the agony of last-minute cancellation. I appealed to wealthy young businessmen who got off on the idea of the craziness of the rock and roll industry. My far-flung career as a rising independent concert promoter was off and running.

I was the first promoter to bring rock and roll back to Carnegie Hall, after it had been banished for several years following the Beatles' historic concert there. I was able to convince Julius Bloom, executive director of Carnegie Hall, that he was culturally segregating a very important part of music, and that Carnegie Hall was a place for all music and all people. I promoted Led Zeppelin, The Byrds, and The Flying Burrito Brothers at Carnegie Hall. I felt that every time I went into a facility that had previously refused rock and roll, it was two points for the good guys.

I was the first person to produce Bette Midler in concert, following her development as a cabaret sensation at the Continental Baths and other underground venues. Together we worked on adapting the sound, lights, and content of her show for the concert stage. It was one of the first and last times that my technical training in theater production from Carnegie Mellon University came into play in my work as a concert promoter. Both Bette Midler concerts I produced, one at Carnegie Hall and the other at Avery Fisher Hall (then Philharmonic Hall) in Lincoln Center, sold out instantly.

In 1969 I began my affiliation with The Rolling Stones by producing two concerts at Madison Square Garden. How did it happen? Incredibly, the Madison Square Garden shows were given to me by The Rolling Stones' agent, the William Morris Agency. Whether I had a secret ally at the William Morris Agency, or whether the political machinations of that era dictated that The Rolling Stones be promoted by Howard Stein instead of by Bill Graham or my major New York competitor for many years, Ron Delsener, is still a mystery. These concerts, until recently, were my greatest claim to fame, and made me, in the music industry at least, something of a cause célèbre.

My principal source of attractions was Premier Talent, the leading rock and roll booking agency in the United States. My major ally for many years was Frank Barsalona, the president and founder of Premier Talent, who traveled on the same airplanes as I did with his first major acts, Herman's Hermits and The Animals. Frank Barsalona funneled virtually every new act he signed into working with me, including Humble Pie, Frampton's Camel, Peter Frampton, Emerson, Lake & Palmer, Yes, and Black Sabbath. I promoted concerts with Jimi Hendrix and Jim Morrison. I promoted Janis Joplin's last concert before her untimely death.

When the Kinetic Playground in Chicago closed, and there was a lot of room for competition in the Chicago market, I went there as a promoter. I moved into Texas, Miami, and Atlanta under the same circumstances. My frequency of concerts increased to the point where Howard Stein Enterprises was handling more than 250 concerts a year. It was too much. Eventually, inevitably, Howard Stein Enterprises went bust.

It was regrettable that I discovered the importance of thinking about the bottom line in promoting concerts just as I was going out of business. I had spread myself too thin. I had neglected looking at the profit and loss sheets for my own concerts, and was doing far too many marginal attractions, biding my time for the authentic superstars who came along only occasionally. I agonized over the smaller profit margins that agencies were allowing concert promoters to make. Finally, dissatisfied with my place in the music business hierarchy, I stopped accepting the rules of this increasingly artist/agency-dominated industry. My punishment was to be frozen out of every major concert promotion opportunity until I was forced to declare bankruptcy.

It took a while to pick up the pieces. I tried personal management, but it wasn't right for me. Luckily, with the aid of my friends, I was able to think through my personal dilemma and discover a way to utilize my entrepreneural talents without having to sacrifice either my personal happiness or profit potential. My new career as one of the managing partners of Xenon, a major New York City discotheque, holds great promise of enabling me to do the things I've always wanted to as a producer. If it succeeds, it will also enable me to attain a level of stature and freedom in the music business that only one concert promoter, Bill Graham, who happened on the scene first, has ever been able to command.

The information in this book may be the wisdom of a fool, but it is factual and correct. It's a new twist in the concert promotion business. It's not sensational, and it's not filled with gossip; rather, it is a behind-the-scenes look at the pure business of concert promotion. If the book has a star, that star is The Truth.

2
The Cast of Characters

IT'S VERY HARD to paint a picture of what the successful concert promoter looks like. What they all have in common is that they're aggressive. They're doers. They don't talk about the theory of promoting a concert. They don't just play with the idea of wanting to be a promoter for years and years. They go out and they do something.

Successful concert promoters are survivors. They don't die after one ruinous concert. They don't fall with one punch. They roll with the setbacks, and they survive.

Concert promoters—both men and women—have lots of chutzpah. They're magicians: that's part of the job. At the last moment, when the show is not going to go on because there's a rainstorm and everyone's about to get electrocuted, somehow the successful promoter pulls a rabbit out of his hat, and the show goes on.

Successful concert promoters are fast thinkers. They have to be. Unlike people in the record or publishing businesses, where events happen over a longer period of time and involve advances and royalties, the concert promoter lives in the present. He's tied to a moment of truth. At 8:00 P.M. on January 23, the night the promoter's show is scheduled to happen, it has to happen. That's the night the promoter makes or loses his money. Concert promoters have to be able to deal with immediate situations. They have to react quickly.

Concert promoters have to be flexible. They have to be able to service their stars—even if the real star is not the artist, but the agent, manager, or record company president. Promoters must appear competent, professional, and satisfied with the work of everyone they deal with. Threatening your stars with your own power drive would be suicidal for most concert promoters.

Successful concert promoters are cagey. Very often, they're sharks, going for the jugular of their competition. Some of them are killers, but only against their competitors. To the agents, the lifeblood of the promotion business, they act quite differently.

Some successful concert promoters are forever apple polishing, constantly playing on the egos of their attractions, the egos of the agents, the egos of managers. Self-pride means nothing to these promoters; getting the act they want means everything.

You don't have to have a college education to be a successful concert promoter. In fact, if you intimidate people by sounding too intellectual or slick, it can work against you. Concert promotion is a very personal business. The various people you work with—managers, clients, agents, roadies, stagehands—expect you to relate to them. IBM may not care whether you're haughty or self-demeaning, but in this business you have to be able to get along with people.

Aside from Margorie Sexton, president of Gulf Artists Productions, who is a very successful concert promoter in the Tampa/St. Petersburg area, I know of no other women who are major concert promoters. However, the way women are perceived by the men in this industry seems consistent with the changing way women are perceived in society. The time is becoming ripe for women to become much more active in the promotion end of the business, and I expect that development to come in the not too distant future.

Age doesn't matter. Some promoters do base a lot of their operating success on the fact that they're young, that they're deeply involved in the music, that they party with the attraction, and that they dress and behave like the performers they are presenting. But there is another school of concert promoters who readily admit they have no interest in the music or, for that matter, the attraction. Concert promoters can be personally divorced from the aesthetics of what they're presenting, but they must be totally married to all the implications of the way rock aesthetics affect the audience.

Concert promoters are crapshooters. The day a concert is booked, everyone involved has certain financial certainties he can rely on—everyone, that is, except the concert promoter. The act knows that it's going to be paid its guarantee, and perhaps its percentage of the profit. The agency knows that it's going to make 10 or 15 percent of that guarantee. The manager of the act knows that he's going to make 10 percent, 20 percent, 30 percent, or more of the act's take. The hall knows that it's going to get its minimum rent. The insurance company knows that it has received its premium. The police (acting as security guards) know that they're going to get paid. The various unions know that they're going to be paid, otherwise they won't permit the show to go on. The box-office treasurer and Ticketron agencies have already paid themselves out of the gross receipts.

Only the concert promoter rolls craps. Everyone else will be paid, but in today's business, unless the concert is a complete sellout, the promoter may wind up with nothing for himself, after he has anted up what his overhead requires to his secretary, production coordinator, stage manager, and landlord.

Add it all up, and you come away with a picture that, for many naive purveyors of careers in the music business, is totally unbelievable. Concert promoters are not very important. They own nothing, unless they own a club. They can easily be replaced. They don't receive advances, royalties, or other forms of annuities. Their job is to service the stars, to cater to the interests of other people more important politically and financially than themselves.

The disproportionate bargaining power of concert promoters compared to the masters they serve—superstars, agents, managers, and halls—underscores today's business in the most fundamental way. Fifteen years ago, when rock and roll first began breaking, it was different. Nobody had all the answers. Agents and artists looked to the local concert promoter as a valuable source of information on what worked best with the audience: what excited them, what they liked, what made them go crazy. Agents and managers didn't realize how valuable attractions like The Rolling Stones, The Who, and Emerson, Lake & Palmer would become. Major artists were booked by promoters at prices that today would be considered comical.

Once the agents and managers had become acclimated to the new audience of rock and roll teenyboppers and had perceived that they could charge virtually whatever they wanted for their superstars, the importance of the promoter dwindled. Concert promoters are no longer on equal footing with agents and managers. Only a major development, such as a class-action suit brought by promoters against artists and agents, or the establishment of a national union of concert promoters—both highly unlikely eventualities—would significantly change this present ordering of roles.

Who are the various players in the concert promotion business, and how important are they? The superstar artist is the most principal player. Without the real superstar—an artist or group of artists (the "attraction") that sells millions of albums and has an international following of diehard fans—the concert promoter has virtually no chance of rolling sevens or elevens back to back over a period of time. Getting the chance to promote superstar artists in major venues should be the goal of every person who has set his sights on becoming a "major" concert promoter.

Next in order to the superstar artists are the godfathers of the concert business: the booking agents. If a major agency is willing to do business with a promoter—an attitude that will be dependent on how many services you perform for the agency and how well you perform them—the promoter will eventually be permitted to showcase superstar artists and make an excellent living. If a major agency is not willing to do business with you, either you have to figure out some way to ingratiate yourself with that agency and make it deliver major talent to you, or face inevitable hard times.

The formidable strength of booking agents is derived from the employment contract they require artist clients to sign. In essence, this document says that the agent an artist signs with has the exclusive right, for the term of the contract, to act as the artist's employment advisor. Concert promoters, motion picture studios, television producers, advertisers, book and music publishers, and sometimes even record companies have been conditioned (often by lawsuits) to negotiate deals with the booking agent, not the artist or the artist's manager. Full-service agents charge their artists fees ranging from 10 to 15 percent of the gross income they receive from all employment sources. Literally thousands of booking agencies exist in the United States, but in reality there are only six U.S. agencies (see appendix A) that control most of the major attractions sought by rock concert promoters. This is a classic case of the seller's market, where the buyers (concert promoters) are many, and the sellers (agents) are few and enormously powerful.

Personal managers can also be very important players in the behind-the-scenes jockeying for superstar artist attractions. The role of the personal manager is to advise the artist how best to develop and package his or her talent. The role of the booking agent is to advise the artist how best to bring that talent to the marketplace. There is a fair amount of overlap between the two jobs of manager and agent, although the exigencies of the twenty-four-hour day force most managers to specialize in developing talent, while most agents specialize in booking talent. Personal managers charge their clients anywhere from 20 percent to 50 percent of the artist's gross income from all sources.

Gingerly approaching this nexus of mutual interests is the independent concert promoter. The role of the concert promoter is to obtain certain prerequisite items needed to present successful concerts: a concert facility, date, cash, his own professional experience, and enough manpower to see the job through.

The concert promoter will negotiate with the facility for use of the hall and a date for the concert; negotiate with the agency for the headliner (superstar) and supporting act(s) that accompany the headliner; purchase tickets and arrange to have them sold at the box office, through ticket brokers, and at Ticketron outlets; coordinate all preproduction activities with the agency, the hall, and the artist's road manager; develop the advertising and publicity campaign in the local marketplace for the concert; supervise the load-in of equipment, sound, and lights on the day of the concert; act as an intermediary between the road manager and stagehands, Teamsters, and other union personnel involved in moving, installing, and maintaining equipment; cater meals for the artist's entourage; greet and occasionally introduce the artist; and be available in the box office at intermission or immediately after the show for an accounting to the artist's representative of actual income received from the concert.

While this is going on, a successful concert promoter is juggling in his mind a half dozen other concerts that are scheduled to happen in the next few days or weeks; plotting to book six more major attractions; and wondering how to cut overhead costs and get home before 4:00 in the morning one night that week. The job involves endless hours, near calamities at every turn, a poor return on the dollar in most cases, and very little contact with the headliner. Concert promoters who survive past the age of fifty can be numbered on the fingers of one hand. Still, if you're lucky, it can be one of the most exhilarating, challenging, and rewarding jobs in the entertainment world.

Undoubtedly, by definition if not by position on the to-tempole, the most important character in the concert promotion business—more important even than the godfather agent, the superstar attraction, or the most prestigious venue in town—is you. The fact that you're reading this book suggests that, to some degree, you're fascinated with the prospects of getting into the concert promotion field. But let me tell you that you will not be able to get into the concert promotion business at anything other than the lowest possible level unless you are fortunate enough to be in the right place at the right time; unless you possess those crap-shooting essentials—charismatic personality, super sales-manship, daring, imagination, and patience—that unfortunately cannot be learned from reading books or by going to school.

The concert promotion business is a business of personalities. Who you know is much more important than what you know, or how well you say it. Developing and maintaining good business relationships with key agents, personal managers, and artists is absolutely essential if you're going to succeed. It's going to take a lot more than memorizing the names, addresses, and telephone numbers of the six leading U.S. agencies in appendix A. It's going to take years of sweat, learning the technical functions of promoting concerts, developing a good reputation, and in other ways "paying your dues" to the industry before you earn a significant break.

The greatest obstacle you will have to overcome is your nonidentity, or lack of industry standing. The agent never wants to have a phone call at 3:00 A.M. from an artist who complains, "How could you have let us play for this flake? We're calling from Wisconsin, and this promoter you sold us to is an amateur. He doesn't have the balance of the money here. When I get back to New York, I'm having my attorney call you, and we're moving from your agency to your leading competitor's agency." Everyone is suspicious of the outsider in this business. Just because you may have money doesn't mean that the problem of getting sellout talent becomes any easier. If you're not known to the inside establishment—if you don't have the track record—you won't be entrusted a major attraction, no matter how much money you offer to spend.

Agents have their own problems. They've got a lot of cities to worry about, and they have a lot of artists to handle. They tend to deal from instinct. They're not graduates of the Harvard School of Business. They play from gut reaction, and they're very protective of their powerful positions. The fact that they deal from instinct does not make them less effective. Some of them are brilliant in their natural music-business perceptions.

This ordering of roles in the concert promotion business should help suggest the process through which enterprising potential concert promoters can start their careers. Look for opportunities to help the booking agent. This can be either by offering to promote concerts for some of the agent's new artists or for artists on bumpy ground (i.e., over-the-hill artists), or by doing concerts in new concert facilities or new cities. Use as your guiding light the precept that if you're not doing something that is of real value to the agent, you're not in the box for future favors. Every major concert you might eventually receive is conditioned on the service you have performed in the line of duty of breaking in new attractions for the agency.

What this has to do with how good you are, how clever you are at promoting concerts, and how ingenius you are at deploying lights, sound, and backstage conveniences, is very much to the point. Agents don't need inventive concert promoters with college degrees. They need people with proven track records for doing what they're told to do, period. In today's business, virtually every conceivable item requiring original thinking has already been thought out—and demanded—in the artist's contract rider. The artist will tell you what beer to order, what size the cans or bottles should be, and at what temperature they should be stored. Requests for wine may come complete with a recommended year of vintage. The promoter will be told whether to meet the artist at the airport in a Lincoln Continental or a Cadillac limousine.

The role of the concert promoter today is to deliver a sellout audience for the artist and the artist's agency. Most deals are predicated on a guarantee plus percentage of gross: in other words, the more seats paid for, the greater the artist/agent's share in the evening's performance.

The best way to insure a sellout is to book a major superstar attraction. Selling out on less than a "sure shot" can happen, but it takes more than a fair amount of luck, and perhaps a very canny concert promoter.

Underneath it all is the basic disparity among artist/king, agent/lord, and promoter/servant. Promoters who presume to be more powerful than they actually are will quickly be silenced, as I was. The promoter, who works so hard, is not assured of anything in today's business. It will be up to you to decide, after I've shared my accumulated knowledge of this field with you, whether you could make a successful future of it in concert promotion.

3

How Promoters Make Their Money

THIS CHAPTER will explain one of the most mystifying elements of the concert promotion business: the process whereby promoters are allowed by the artist/agent to make their profits.

At the bottom of the barrel—the agency's unknown, newly signed talent—there is at least a sense of parity. These acts will make their professional debuts in small clubs, rather than concert halls. Especially at this start-up level of the business, the knowledgeable agent is concerned that the facility doesn't overpower or intimidate the artist and that the artist plays to an enthusiastic, albeit small, gathering of people.

Exposure, not windfall profits, is what the agency wants for its new, unknown artists. Club dates for an entire week can be negotiated by the club owner at fees as low as $500 for the week, two shows a night. If the club has a regular clientele, or the artist's record company buys up all the seats in order to insure favorable newspaper reviews (e.g., "Last night, [record company's] new attraction played to a wild, standing-room-only crowd"), the club owner can do quite well selling tickets, drinks, and food.

Once beyond the small club, the agency tightens the screws on the promoter, first in small increments, then in ever-increasing demands for more control, more money, more everything. The financial formula for rock attractions who graduate from the club circuit is that: (1) they are entitled to a nonrefundable guarantee, half to be paid "up front," on signing the contract, and half to be paid on the day of the concert, prior to the artist's actually performing; and (2) they may be entitled to a percentage of the gross income, less applicable taxes, derived from ticket sales. This percentage, exercised at the discretion of the agency, is referred to in the industry as the PC.

Guarantee figures reflect what the agency feels the act is worth in the marketplace that season, based on record sales, television appearances, motion pictures, and the attraction's general fame. Guarantees, as a rule, are not negotiable in today's business. If the agency tells you, "This attraction costs $1,500 flat, and if the show sells out the act receives a $750 bonus" (a common practice in the industry), that's it. Most opening acts will play for flat fees, unless they are legitimate major artists—then you can be sure the agent will want a guarantee plus PC.

Quite a few middle-level acts, somewhere between start-up attractions and superstars, will also play for flat guarantees. Peter Frampton, at one time, played for flat guarantees, first $1,000, then $1,500, then $4,000 a show and up. Agents may still be willing to trade exposure for profits with middle-level acts, but promoters must be very careful which acts they choose. If the attraction doesn't fill the concert hall, the promoter is bound to take a beating financially and to lose favor with the act, the agency, and the artist's manager. On the other hand, if the act does well with the promoter, and is flourishing throughout the rest of the country, its costs for the next concert will probably escalate to include a PC.

The artist's percentage will change based on the size of the venue that is being used for the concert. The PC at a 5,000-seater will be greater than the PC at an outdoor 100,000-seater, where the volume of potential ticket buyers may result in a seven-figure gate. For middle-level acts the PC may be in the area of 40 to 60 percent of the gross ticket income after break-even (which figure includes the artist's guarantee, facility rent, total production costs, and taxes). For superstars, the PC may be 90 percent of the gross ticket income after break-even, or more.

Now for the promoter. Dealing with acts at the superstar level, promoters will most certainly be restricted to a small percentage—anywhere from 10 to 15 percent of the concert's gross ticket income after break-even, less applicable taxes. At lower levels, the promoter may be able to make slightly more percentage points, or at least get most of his concerts tilted toward the upper range (14–17 percent) rather than the lower (10–12.5 percent). But the days when promoters could pay flat fees to a superstar, or flat fees plus one-half of the overage, or excess income beyond break-even, are long gone. The key to making money as a promoter is to negotiate your percentage payment as soon after a particular concert's break-even point has been achieved as possible. Otherwise, if the concert is not a sellout, the promoter may walk away with nothing.

The following hypothetical situation illustrates this key concept. A concert has a gross potential, or GP, of $95,000 after taxes (i.e., if 100 percent of the tickets to the concert are sold at the face value of the tickets, it will gross $95,000 after taxes have been paid). The attraction is getting a $25,000 guarantee, plus a 90 percent PC. The agent notifies the promoter that he will be allowed to make 10 percent of the gross ticket income after taxes (the promoter's PC), but only in the event the concert sells out. In other words, if the promoter sells every ticket for the concert, his maximum profit is $9,500.

Let's say this concert costs an additional $50,000 to produce. The total cost of promoting the concert, including talent, facility rent, other miscellaneous production costs, and taxes, equals $75,000. Out of the remaining $25,000, the promoter expects to receive $9,500.

Here is the catch. The deal with the agent says that only in the event of a sellout will the promoter receive $9,500. If the hall has 90 percent seats sold, the promoter won't get $9,500. If the hall has 85 percent seats sold, the promoter will get less than he would have for a 90 percent capacity house. The way this works is that the agent will usually permit the promoter to take only one-half of his potential earnings immediately after break-even (in this case, $75,000). The $4,500 between $75,000 and $79,500 goes to the promoter as immediate payment; thereafter the promoter will receive something on the order of one-third of the additional aftertax income between $79,500 and whatever amount of money is collected for the concert.

In this case, if the concert played to an 85 percent capacity house grossing $80,750 after taxes, and the promoter received one-third of the overage beyond $79,500 (or one-third of $1,250), the promoter would make $4,916 total ($4,500 plus $416). If the concert played to a 90 percent capacity house, the promoter would make $6,500. If the concert played to a 95 percent capacity house, the promoter would make $8,083. Only if the concert was a complete sellout would the promoter receive $9,500.

By the same token, if the concert played to a 75 percent capacity house, the promoter would be out of pocket $3,750. He would only have taken in $71,250, and the concert cost $75,000 to produce. If you ever actually promote a major concert where 75 percent of your potential audience shows up, which can be a lot of people, then discover that for being 75 percent successful you've actually lost $3,750, you will be closer to the almost constant agony of being a major rock and roll concert promoter. Unless you're able to present consistent sellout talent on some regular basis, you can't possibly make money. Huge sums will pass through your hands like butter. Everyone else but you will be paid. It is a maddening, unfortunate situation, and there's nothing any promoter, especially the start-up variety, can do to change it. The artist, through his agent, calls the shots. If you want the chance of becoming a major concert promoter and working with sure sellout attractions, you have no choice but to accept these terms of employment.

I would hasten to add that, on a per-concert basis, the agent's practice of holding back at least part of the promoter's PC immediately after break-even makes sense. If a concert sold out quickly, and the promoter knew he was going to receive 100 percent of his profit immediately after break-even, his incentive to continue working on that concert would be gone. The concert might go on with less than the total professional support it needs from the promoter and his staff. Using the split-payment approach, the agent can continue dangling his financial carrot in front of the promoter up to and through the completion of the show.

Even though the concept of split payments has merit, I would nevertheless encourage start-up promoters to try to negotiate as much of their PC immediately after break-even as they can. If the agent offers 50 percent after break-even, ask for 60 percent. If the agent offers 60 percent, ask for 65 or 70 percent. This is the last remaining area for negotiation between a concert promoter and a major booking agency in the rock and roll concert performance business. This is where promoters make their money: the sooner you make your money after break-even, and the more money you make, the better it is for you as a concert promoter.

I imagine that quite a few readers are expecting more than this perfunctory analysis of negotiating the price of talent, which in turn affects the promoter's profit. Believe me, there's not much more to be said. Big-league concert promotion does not tolerate hemming and hawing over price. Several months before a major act is ready to go out on tour, the major booking agency of that act will notify the major concert promoters around the country that a tour is taking shape. Does the promoter wish to promote the attraction at the major facility in town? Usually the answer is yes. The promoter may ask, "Is it possible for me to promote other concerts in other cities for this attraction?" If the promoter is held in great esteesm by the attraction's agent, the answer may be yes; otherwise, it will be a firm no.

The agent will then tell the promoter what the artist's guarantee and PC will be, and when the attraction wishes to perform at that facility. The promoter has a few hours to contact the facility, find out if dates are available, and compute the GP for this potential concert. This exercise, which involves a determination of how many seats there are in the facility, and how much to charge for tickets in the orchestra, loge, and balconies, is called "scaling the house."

If the promoter thinks he can come out ahead on the concert, the deal is set. If the promoter doesn't think he can come out ahead, either because the act isn't that strong in his market or because the price of the talent is too high, he'll pass. Nobody argues over guarantees or artist PCs in this "gentleman's" business, where the players know each other so well. The promoter's chief concern is when he's going to be paid. Negotiations about that detail, in my experience, are usually five-minute affairs during which the promoter reminds the agent of his past service record with that agency. Ultimately, it is the agency that either accepts or rejects the promoter's payment scheme.

Deals influencing the price of an attraction can be worked out with smaller agencies, but these are Pyrrhic victories for the promoter. If the act doesn't have a name, it won't sell tickets. The best deal in the world on paper is meaningless if the promoter's concert doesn't have the true potential of selling out. Being able to get major talent, as we shall see, is the most important success ingredient in becoming an established concert promoter.

Here are some practical suggestions relating to potential profits. Keep your office overhead costs down. In fact, don't even have an office. Work out of your home or apartment. All you need to be in the promotion business is a table, a chair , and a working telephone. Save whatever profits you make for better things than paying rent.

One of the most dangerous parts of the concert promotion business has to do with what I call over-the-hill artists. These attractions, who may have been authentic superstars several years ago, can no longer command exorbitant fees. Still, they will expect—and their contract riders will demand—deluxe treatment by the promoter. When you reach the stage of talking with important agents about major attractions, they will undoubtedly ask you first to promote some of their over-the-hill acts. I would stress to the agent that you know the attraction is no longer one of the top twenty acts in the country, and that chances of a sellout are not great. Ask 20 percent of the GP after taxes for yourself, with 60 or 70 percent of the promoter's PC payable immediately after break-even. Smart agents recognize that promoters, too, must have an incentive to be in this business. If you ask properly, and can offer the agent a persuasive argument for your receiving as much as 20 percent of the GP after taxes, you may be able to come away from these trial affairs in a financially sound condition.

Your creditworthiness may be investigated by the booking agency as a precondition for doing business with that agency. If you're not financially sound, you're not ready to seek talent from a major booking agency, regardless of how little that talent costs.

The common practice in the trade, as I've already stated, is for the promoter to pay 50 percent of the talent's guarantee up front, usually by certified check. However, if you are a brand new promoter, you may be asked to pay the entire guarantee up front.

Finally, it is important to know your place. The promoter's job involves servicing not only the artist, but the artist's production dictates. If the artist wishes to use his own sound and light equipment, the promoter can't argue that he can obtain the same equipment from a local supplier for half of what the artist is charging him. Giving the artist whatever he wants is the price of admission for promoting major rock concerts. It's no longer possible to cut corners. With the right artist and the right facility, it still is possible for the promoter to make a handsome living, but only after many years of service to the industry. Whether it's worth it, even to the top concert promoters in the United States, is a subject to think about very seriously.

4

Getting Talent

DELIVERABILITY: that's the key to becoming a successful concert promoter. Deliverability to you, by the agency, of an attraction. Having the attraction play for you, as opposed to the already established concert promoter. Those who have made any attempt at this realize how near-to-impossible it is for the novice to break the bonds that exist between the present buyers and sellers of talent.

However, there is a way to get your foot in the door that does not involve miracles. It means dealing with the realities of the concert promotion business: being patient, dedicated, and willing to sacrifice financially for several, perhaps many, years. If you really want it, and you're talented and lucky, it can be done.

I think the most important thing for the reader to realize is what a task it's going to be to get talent—how frustrating it's going to be. Inevitably, one starts to feel paranoid that the industry is not responding to "my" interest, "my" enthusiasm, or to "me" as a person. Everybody—every novice promoter, and I was no exception—has to pay his dues this way. We start by trying to shake an apple off a tree. If we persevere, eventually the agency is going to recognize our legitimate interest in promoting concerts.

I would recommend that before you call to discuss a specific engagement, try to have an initial meeting with an agent (not the president of the agency) in his office. Office appointments are better than meeting backstage or at a party, unless you're at a small party with someone who is well connected with the agent and who can make a personal introduction for you.

Receptionists and secretaries, who command the telephones and therefore control communications between the agent and the outside world, can be extremely important to your overall chances of getting an appointment. These are the people, often inundated with requests, who will first present your case to their boss. Try to become a face or a person to the secretary, as opposed to being merely another voice over the telephone, or another aspiring concert promoter on paper. If you're able to, go to the agency's office and hand-deliver your information. A secretary who's on your side and has the ear of a line agent can make a big difference.

Don't talk to personal managers or artists at the outset of your promotion career. Later on, your relationships with managers and artists may be strong enough for you to deal with them directly. But initially, you must deal with the artist's agent exclusively. If you try to cut out the agency at first, your negotiations will probably backfire to such an extent that you'll be frozen out of the promotion business for a long, long time.

An agent doesn't need another potential buyer calling up for Crosby, Stills & Nash, The Eagles, or Linda Ronstadt. That's not the agent's problem. The agent's problem is finding work for the new attractions that the agency has signed. As a start-up promoter, your potential value to the agency will be determined by whether you are interested in and have the capability of promoting concerts for the agency's new attractions.

The best way to learn about new developments in the music business, if you're a total outsider, is by reading the trade papers: *Billboard, Cashbox, Record World, Radio & Records, Variety,* and *Amusement Business*. Pay particular attention to captioned photographs announcing the recent signing by record companies of unknown artists. Once an artist has been signed to a major record company, it is usually a matter of days or weeks before that artist is also signed to a major booking agency. By contacting the record company, or reading the trades for additional information on which agency the artist signed with, you may be able to get a head start on other promoters seeking to gain admittance at that particular agency.

Explain to the agent in your initial appointment that you're a new promoter, that you don't expect to be laden with gifts of superstars at the outset of the relationship, and that you're willing to serve a function for the agency by promoting its new attractions if the agency, in turn, can be influential in developing your career as a concert promoter. In the initial meeting you should discuss the kinds of attractions the agency has, the agency's conditions for dealing with the promoter, and what kind of service the agency expects from the promoter. It is very important for the promoter to make the agent feel comfortable with him as a business person. Personal references, trial balance sheets for projected concerts involving the agency's attractions, and a copy of the promoter's rental agreement with the facility can be very reassuring signs, to the agent, of the promoter's professionalism.

I would also, in the initial meeting, try to impress the agent with the fact that not only are you enthusiastic and willing to play a developmental role (a key concept) in the careers of their new acts, but that you are financially prepared to handle the burdens of being in business. Don't make an offer, get an acceptance, and then tell the agent that you're going to try to raise the money to produce the show. Have your finances at least partially nailed down before you go there.

Make sure you know what you're talking about. The easiest way for somebody to dismiss you mentally, from a business standpoint, is to consider you a flake—someone who has no idea what he's talking about, or who doesn't know the realities of the business. When the agent asks, "Is there a PC involved?" you should know that PC means percentage. When the agent talks about the GP, you should know that GP is the gross potential of the concert. When the agent asks for ticket prices, you should know how to scale the house, and how many seats there are in the facility. When the agent asks about taxes, you should know what types and percentages these taxes will be.

You must sound like a professional. If you write, which I don't recommend, you must write like a professional. The least you can do is impress the potential seller, the agent, with your comfort within the industry, your knowledge of it, and your fluency with its terminology.

The right person to talk to in this initial meeting is any agent you can get to see. It doesn't have to be the president of the agency. In fact, it's absurd even to think that you'll be able to see the president. Get in to see an agent. Break the ice. Try to get through. Get somebody there to respond to you.

After the initial meeting has been concluded, it's not necessary to have any written correspondence between the promoter and the agent to memorialize the meeting. This is a telephone industry. Try to develop telephone relationships rather than written ones. This is a very valuable thing for a new promoter: to be able to call an agency and have that call taken, instead of waiting for three days for a call to come back to you. Aside from contracts, it's all done on the phone. Deals are confirmed or turned down verbally in the concert promotion business, long before they've gone to contract.

After the intitial meeting, the next step will be a discussion, either in person or on the telephone, concerning a specific concert proposal. While it is essential to have certain data and financial information available on the GP, less applicable taxes, the seating capacity of the facility, and the cost for you to promote the concert, less talent and other variables, you're still not "in" with the agency. You will have to do a second selling job of yourself, your facility, and your services before the agency will award you its talent.

Good halls, in my experience, make very persuasive arguments for aspiring concert promoters. If you think you have the best hall in town for the artist you're attempting to promote, let the agent know it. Be able to describe the hall physically. Give the agent some idea who's played there before, and how successful those attractions were in that facility. Let the agent know who's playing near you, so that the agency doesn't think there's somebody coming in who's going to share your business. Try to explain, if you're already promoting concerts, that you're not playing anybody with a similar audience during that period of time, and that, to the best of your knowledge, none of your local competitors have booked similar attractions.

If the facility is really hot, and anything presented there is a sellout, bring along some newspaper clips or magazine stories about the hall. In short, stress the merits of the hall to the agent: who's played there, how the hall has been used in the past, and the success of the hall with the local audience.

You're not going to impress an agent by saying, "You know that opening act you have that's playing 500-seaters? Well, I believe in it so much that I'm going to put it in a

3,000-seater." Unless the agency wants to destroy you—and
good agencies don't—they're going to think that's absurd.
Smart agencies never want their acts to do badly. They
especially don't want an attraction to develop the reputation of playing to empty auditoriums—of being a "loser" or
a "dead act." If it's a new act and you're offering to headline
them, the agency will want the act to headline in a small
place where the business will at least be hearty. Good exposure, with the possiblility of a turnaway crowd, is much
more desirable to an experienced agent than the lure of
quick money.

As I've already explained, the price of the act is not
negotiable, even for start-up attractions. Either you take it
or you leave it. The real key—and I can't emphasize it
strongly enough—is how you, as opposed to somebody else,
are going to get the attraction. What can you do to influence the agency's decision, so that eventually you will be
able to promote their major attractions?

You're not going to get it by beating the price. Even when
I competed with Ron Delsener, who is presently the major
New York City concert promoter, there weren't more than
three shows out of the hundreds and hundreds we did a year
that Ron Delsener would take from me, or I would take
from him, because one of us was willing to pay more. It
never was that. It was, instead: who deserves the act? Who
should be playing the act? Who put his dues in with that
act? Who worked with that agency? Who's willing to do
more for that agency? Who's willing to commit himself
more to that act?

If price were the only problem involved in getting talent,
then the entire concert promotion industry would be the
loser. We'd all have to be crazy to overpay attractions and
fight against each other, at least in terms of financial return.
Successful promoters get talent because of their abilities,
and because of what they did for the agency in the act's ear-

ly stages. You just hope, although there's no guarantee, that the agency will remember. You also hope that the attraction will remember, too.

This is why promoters can be such backstabbers against their competitors. After the show, which the promoter doesn't own, after the money, which the promoter will spend, he has nothing except his relationships with artists, agents, and managers. These relationships are the promoter's only tangible asset. If they change, he's out of business. If someone else comes in and creates a similar relationship, his business can be halved. The cutthroat nature of this business stems from the promoter's vital concern for protecting that next telephone call to the agency.

Sometimes it is the facility that decides which start-up promoter an agent will work with. Large facilities that draw sellout audiences translate into acceptable GPs for the attraction and the agency. If the promoter can somehow obtain control of an important facility (in the trade we call this an exclusivity), he must be taken seriously by the agent. Even so, if you're able to command a facility, you're not home free. You must be willing to serve the agency. You must be willing to promote whatever acts the agency wants promoted for at least a trial period. If you don't treat the agent with respect, he will either wait for another arena to be built in your city, or look to the surrounding suburbs.

How do you insure that your relationship with the agency will continue, and that eventually you will receive bigger attractions? By doing everything the way the agency wants you to do it. It may sound like pandering, but it's reality. If you have an engagement and you're required to send the agency a 50 percent deposit by certified check by March 15, make sure it gets there and is certified on time.

Don't surprise the attraction. Know the artist's concert rider backwards and forwards, and don't make any changes in it. If the rider states that the attraction is to receive four bottles of this wine and three cases of this beer, don't assume that you can replace "this beer" with "that beer." Don't assume that you can replace meat with cheese. Give the artist exactly what he wants.

Be there during the engagement. Make your presence known. You are the person the attraction is working for, and they want to see you working. They want to see your personal involvement.

You're usually not going to be the person who selects, or packages, the opening act talent that complements the headliner. You're usually going to have a package of two or more artists thrust upon you by the agency. More than likely, in order for you to have a headline attraction, the agency will tell you that you must expose another one of its new acts. Occasionally, when the agency doesn't have another suitable act available, they may let you go to another agency. It's more likely, however, that the headliner's agency will make the call for you: they want the supporting act's agency to feel that "Your agency owes my agency one act."

Expect to lose money over a certain number of start-up concerts when you start promoting. Chances of losing money are much greater with your early shows than with your later ones, when you've learned which advertising media work best and how many production personnel you actually need. But you never stop losing money as a promoter. There's always some favor you have to do that will hurt you in the pocketbook.

When you've figured out what your costs will be after the agent quotes you a price for the attraction, you may realize that the price is at a level where it's impossible for you to make a profit. Be forthright about it with the agent; tell him, "It's impossible for me to make a profit this way." If the agent answers, "We'd like you to do this for us, and in return we will start to give you acts that can make you some money," you have to determine if: (1) you're talking to an agent who has the authority to keep his word; and (2) it's a prudent business gamble.

Concert promotion is a business in which you're very often asked to lose money, or to do something that will more than likely lose money, on a handshake, on a verbal promise, on a nonlegal basis, on the provision that "We'll [the agency] make it up to you." You can't ask for anything in writing—you won't get it. You're constantly negotiating deliverability, not price. You're negotiating with an agent to become their promoter: to become a service arm of that agency. That's the magic.

You always seem to be dealing, in actuality, with future concerts. You're negotiating for the right to do a future concert with a bigger attraction than the one you're talking about. Each concert you do is going to have some bearing on the ones you get next, or the ones that you don't get next.

Even though it's a futures business, make sure, at the end of the year, that you've made more money than you've lost. There's a point where developing a relationship with a developing attraction should stop, and that's the end of the year, the bottom line. Evaluate your position carefully. You are not in business just to develop acts for agents and managers. You are in the concert promotion business to make money for yourself.

5

Costing Out the Show

THERE IS a certain amount of "Which comes first, the chicken or the egg?" thinking required to formulate a logical way to teach concert promotion. I've opted for the view that unless you have the talent to be a promoter, access to the industry, working capital, and an inordinate amount of luck, the need to learn how actually to produce a concert becomes a matter of academic curiosity.

Paradoxically, it has no doubt become evident to the discerning reader that in order to get into the business, raise money, and impress people with your knowledge of the industry, it is essential to have a great deal of financial information relating to the specific concert you wish to promote. Appendix B contains a Production Cost Analysis (PCA) form—a relatively short outline of anticipated expenses likely to be incurred in producing a concert. You may wish to refer to it throughout the discussion in this chapter. It summarizes more than ten years of my working experience as a major concert promoter. If, by using it, you are impressed with the importance of thinking bottom line at every turn, I will be pleased. I know it will save you many of the agonizing mistakes that I, and other promoters before me, made in the absence of an intelligent budgetary planning tool.

The PCA form begins with a listing of key concert elements. The Attraction is simply the headliner that you're playing. Support are all the other attractions that are playing beneath the Attraction: the opening act, or second, third, and fourth acts, if it's an outdoor festival concert. (Note that the PCA is a per-show form, not a per-act form. It is not necessary to fill out a different PCA for each attraction on the show.)

Place is the location of the concert. Date and Time are the date and time of the concert. Weather is an item for future planning. After the concert you might want to say, "It was cold and rainy—perhaps that's why we did 80 percent of sellout," or "Our business was affected by a snowstorm," or "There was a snowstorm that did not affect our business." This is one of the PCA entries that should be filled in after the concert is completed.

Seating Capacity is the number of seats in the facility that you are going to put on sale. It is not necessarily the same number as how many seats actually are in the facility, for the following reasons: (1) the attraction's audio mixing platform, usually positioned in the orchestra section, will require that several rows of seats be cordoned off; (2) if the attraction has bulky onstage sound and light equipment, it may cut off sightlines to the stage in certain sections of the hall; unless you want to contend with unhappy customers, it's best not to put these seats on sale; (3) the attraction may ask for fifty or more complimentary tickets for personal use; (4) the facility, for security and public relations reasons, may also require a large block of free tickets. Every seat the promoter loses from a performance is lost potential revenue.

Make sure you know how many seats the attraction and the facility are going to require prior to filling in Seating Capacity. Ask the attraction's road manager whether sections of the facility other than the orchestra area, where the mixing platform is installed, need to be closed. If the average price of your seats is $7.00, every one hundred seats you lose are worth $700. Don't let your actual seating capacity be a last-minute surprise. **2058328**

Ticket Prices are not controlled by the promoter; they are controlled by competition. This is a very important concept to learn. Regardless of the expense of the concert, the promoter is only going to be able to charge as much as (or less than) his competitors charge for tickets. The audience won't come if you charge more, unless you're offering a supercolossal, extraordinary event. The best way to determine what price your tickets should sell for is to look at your competition. See what they're charging for similar events, and charge those prices. Get hold of the seating arrangement for the facility you're using, and scale the house accordingly. Orchestra and box seats are usually the most expensive; balcony seats cost less. For further information about seating plans, consult with the facility manager.

Gross Potential is simply the amount of dollars that can be taken in if every last available seat were sold. After determining what competition will permit you to sell your tickets for, simply multiply the number of seats in each price category by the unit price of that seat, add the different price areas together, and arrive at the GP. The entry Less Taxes is used in cases where the facility charges direct federal, state, and local taxes to the promoter (many facilities disguise tax payments by offering a flat fee to the promoter, from which they make their quarterly payments to the tax authorities). Potential promoters must quickly get into the habit of finding out their tax liabilities *before* the event takes place, not afterward.

GP Less Taxes is the promoter's net gross potential from the concert if every seat is sold at the ticket price levels you've established. You can't collect more money from the concert than this figure. You stand a very good chance, especially as a start-up concert promoter, of collecting considerably less.

Underneath GP Less Taxes, I've organized the PCA form into line-by-line entries of specific production costs, along with a four-column work area headed Budget, Advanced, Actual, and Variance. Budget is what you budget the expense item to be on paper. Budget figures are determined by shopping around for the best price, most reliable service, or a combination of the two from limousine services, caterers, ticket printers, and the myriad other suppliers of production materiel. Advanced is the amount of money that has to be laid out by the promoter to secure that materiel prior to the concert. Actual is used to record the actual price of the specific items required for the production. Variance is used to record the difference between what the promoter budgeted the item's cost to be, and what it actually cost the promoter to obtain. Matching budget costs against actual costs at the completion of the concert is an excellent way for start-up promoters to gauge their abilities to budget properly and hold costs down to established levels.

First in order of priority among actual production expenses is the Headliner. After the agent has quoted the promoter a price for the headliner, the promoter will enter two figures on the PCA form. Headliner—Guarantee is the non-refundable, guaranteed money the headline attraction is to receive, regardless of how many people attend the concert. Headliner—PC is the amount of additional dollars the headline attraction would receive if the concert is a total sellout, less applicable taxes. There is no guarantee, of course, that the concert will be completely sold, but in terms of budgeting out a concert the promoter should always allow for the greatest bite into his potential profit. When the promoter submits his 50 percent deposit to secure the headliner's services, this amount should be entered in the Advanced column for Headliner—Guarantee.

After the headliner, I like to get all my other talent costs out of the way. In today's business, many support acts also receive headliner-like deals involving guarantees and a PC, or overage, beyond break-even. The PCA form provides space for Support—Guarantee and Support—PC. Once again the promoter should allow for a total sellout in computing Support—PC.

I've learned to leave room for additional attractions, or last-minute substitutions. Opening Acts and Third and Fourth acts, often used in outdoor festivals, usually get only guarantees. They may, however, receive bonuses if the concert does extremely well, or if they deserve them. If, for example, you need to use the Opening Act—Guarantee/Bonus line, include the bonus in your computations. Always give yourself the outside figure. If you're going to be surprised, be pleasantly surprised that the concert didn't cost you as much money as you budgeted for it.

The final entry under Talent, Local Musicians, should not be confused with payments to the headliner's backup musicians, or the support attraction's backup musicians. Backup musicians are paid directly by the headliner and support attractions out of the guarantee and PC they receive from the promoter (or else they're on straight salary to the attraction). Local Musician payments involve facilities throughout the United States that charge the promoter for musicians affiliated with the local musicians union. At Madison Square Garden, for example, the promoter must pay Local 802, American Federation of Musicians, a musicians guarantee of $250 per concert. It's not a lot of money. It is a highly questionable practice, however, since the union players are never called on to work and sometimes are not even in attendance. Find out if the facility charges a musicians guarantee, complain if you must, but include it in your budget.

The word Other punctuates the PCA form as a constant reminder, to you and me, that no matter how experienced you are, there's something you may have overlooked, some new wrinkle in the carpet. Learn to expect surprises.

Tickets, the next heading on the PCA form, can either be a thorn in the side of the budget-conscious concert promoter, or the easiest item to fill out on the entire form. If the promoter is using regular printed tickets (in the trade we call them hard tickets), their price can easily and specifically be obtained from one or more ticket printers that the facility works with on a regular basis. If the tickets are sold exclusively at the facility's box office, merely enter the price of printing the hard tickets on the PCA form at Printing, and you're home free.

However, most tickets aren't sold exclusively at one location. Hard tickets may be given to ticket brokers for distribution to ticket outlets located throughout a metropolitan area.

Ticketron, the computerized ticket service, extends even further the convenience of purchasing tickets away from the facility's box office. The promoter must pay additional charges for this convenience. Ticket agencies charge anywhere from 3 to 5 percent of their gross collections, less applicable taxes. Ticketron charges vary from $.25 to $.50 per ticket, depending on which part of the country you're in.

The best source of information on where people buy tickets is the box-office treasurer's ticket manifest. Most facilities furnish this manifest to the promoter at the completion of the concert: it itemizes all ticket sales by category, including box office, mail order, ticket agency, and Ticketron. By matching your headliner's audience with the audience for similar attractions, it is possible for start-up promoters to project what percentage of ticket sales will come through the various ticket sources. It may not be possible for you to gain direct access to an actual ticket manifest. The information you want, however, is easy enough to get from a concerned booking agent or facility manager.

Next, the promoter has to establish contact with the Ticketron salesman in his town, and contact several leading ticket agencies for the best possible deal. The facility manager should be able to help with referrals. Both Ticketron and the ticket agencies deduct their service charge directly from gross collections, and pass the balance on to the promoter.

Don't take ticket charges lightly. If you have a 7,500-seater coming up, and you project that 30 percent of your audience (2,250 people) will buy tickets through Ticketron, and Ticketron is charging you $.50 per ticket, you would have to enter $1,125 on the PCA form at Ticketron. For the same concert, if you project that 20 percent of your audience (1,500 people) will buy tickets through ticket agencies, and the average price of a ticket is $6.00, and the ticket agency is charging you 5 percent, you would have to enter $450 on the PCA form at Distribution. Only at the outer ends of the business—the 250-seaters featuring unknown artists, or the Madison Square Garden concert featuring The Who—is it possible to avoid paying service charges for ticket distribution. The Who will sell out in a matter of hours at the box office. The 250-seater will be lucky to have a dozen off-the-street customers pay money at the box office, though the seats may be occupied by friends of the artist (freebies), or paid for by an obliging record company.

The next section of the PCA form, Facility, starts off with headliner-like computations for the facility rent. If the promoter is being charged a flat fee, use the Facility Rental—Guarantee line. If the promoter is being charged a guarantee against PC, whichever is greater, use the Facility Rental—PC line—this will be the outside figure. In my experience, facilities charge anywhere from 12 to 22.5 percent of GP, less applicable taxes, if they opt for their own PC.

Underneath Facility Rental I begin listing all the expense items that I've ever dealt with for producing concerts. Many of these items may be included in the promoter's rental agreement with the facility. Many may not be required for a particular show. Still, it's better to know whether there might be hidden charges related to your concert, or costs the novice promoter might overlook. I am going to explain briefly each of the items contained in the PCA form. The best way to ascertain whether you will be charged for these items is to contact the facility manager by phone, use the PCA form as a checklist, and ask, "Am I going to be charged for the House Manager?" "Am I going to have to pay for the Ushers?" "Is the Police Department my responsibility, or yours?" and so on. Read your facility contract carefully, but do ask questions.

The House Manager is the person responsible for everything that goes on in the facility, except the stage and backstage areas, which are the responsibility of the union steward. The Assistant House Manager is the second man in charge, after the House Manager. Company Managers and General Managers, in my experience, are only involved in Broadway productions, where the contracts are of a different nature than those with clubs or with large arenas. They act as negotiators between the promoter and the various unions, contractors, and concessionaires who want the promoter's business. The provide production assistance to the promoter, but are themselves unionized personnel.

The Ushers are the people that seat you at a concert. Directors are simply head ushers. If seats for the concert you're promoting are on a first-come, first-served basis (unreserved seating), or if it's an outdoor festival show, you do not need ushers and directors.

Ticket Takers are the people who take your tickets, tear them in half, give you back the stub of the ticket, and (you hope) slide the other half into a big box for later accounting.

Internal Security are the crowd control people who work indoors. External Security are the crowd control people who work outdoors. Both security forces are employed by the facility, not the Police Department, which is autonomous. It is important to find out how many security people the facility intends to use for your concert and what their hourly rate is.

The Police Department is an economic variable in terms of promoting concerts. In New York City, where I've done most of my shows, it is against the law for a cop to moonlight in a security role. Police are therefore assigned to concert duty as part of their public safety program and don't cost the promoter anything. In almost every other city I've worked in, however, police do get paid by the promoter for working concerts. In either case, the facility will tell the promoter how many police to use for a particular event. Again, find out how many police are scheduled to be used and the hourly rate they charge (including overtime) for concert security.

Electricity/Heat is a reminder that some halls may want to pass on a portion of their overhead expenses to the promoter. I never had to pay it, but I know it's not impossible. It's definitely something you should ask about up front.

There are occasions when the promoter is required to pay a flat fee for the use of Air Conditioning in the facility on the night of the concert. I'm sure the fee has gone up since the last time I had to pay this ($100) at the Houston Astrodome.

The only time I've ever had to pay a Water/Sewerage fee was when I did a show at Shea Stadium. Plumbing is one item that has to be working at a major concert. You hope that the plumbers union in your town won't ask for it, but if you're required to pay a Water/Sewerage fee, you don't have much choice.

Under Box Office, the Treasurer is the person in charge of selling tickets. The Assistant Treasurer is the second in command. Ticket Sellers are self-explanatory. Their fees are very predictable, since in most facilities these are union jobs.

The Telephone Person answers the facility's ticket information phone, informing potential customers that "Jethro Tull will be here on October 3 at 8:00 P.M. Tickets are $9.00, $8.00, and $7.00. We still have these tickets available through mail order or Ticketron." Sometimes there is a $50 or $100 charge for this Telephone Person. There may also be a slight service charge for using the box-office Telephone for outgoing calls.

If tickets are being sold through the mail, the facility will charge the promoter for Stamps and Envelopes. By checking ticket manifests for headliner attractions similar to yours, you should be able to estimate what percentage of business will come through mail order, and determine how much money to budget for postage.

Maintenance, the upkeep of the facility, is usually included in the facility rent, although on occasion I have been charged as much as $750 for maintenance services. If the promoter owns his own facility, there will be greater need for the PCA maintenance check-off list. In any case, I think it would be instructive to define these maintenance cost items.

The Janitor is the person who oversees the mechanical operations (plumbing, heating, and so on) of the facility. The Porters are the people who clean up the place. Valets are men assigned to work in the Men's Room. Matrons are women assigned to work in the Ladies' Room. For certain headliners, valets and matrons will be replaced by members of the Police Department.

The Exterminator, in this instance, refers to insect control, not enemies. Holmes Security is an example of the professional independent security services that exist in virtually every major U.S. city. Their job is to patrol the inside and outside of the facility and prevent vandalism.

Cartage is the cost of garbage collection and removal. Supplies could be T-shirts or flashlights for the facility's security or ushers, as well as light bulbs, spotlight gels, and wiring, if you own your own facility. Repairs covers the chairs that break, the mechanical piece that goes out, and any general repair work needed to keep the facility operational.

Upkeep is the shampooing of rugs, changing of the stage floor each year—whatever will keep the facility alive, clean, and fresh.

Engineers and Handymen are people who specialize in taking care of the facility's boiler system, air conditioning, and electrical system.

The next major area of the PCA form, Production, covers the physical staging of the show. Production estimates, in my experience, always come in too low, even if you ask for outside figures. I strongly recommend adding 15 percent to whatever cost estimates you receive for any of the expense items covered in Production.

If you're not using a proscenium theater, or one built with a permanent stage, you will be required by the attraction to construct a stage, or to rent the attraction's own portable stage. Most facilities charge the promoter for Stage Construction. The cost, in my experience, is anywhere from $1,000 to $2,500. Find out from the booking agent how many hours it takes to construct the headliner's stage under normal working conditions, then contact the facility manager and see how much time you will have to put the stage together. If set-up time is short, you're going to need additional labor to compensate. Don't forget to add 15 percent to the outside estimate you receive from the facility manager.

If the facility does not have permanent chairs in the orchestra section (multipurpose sports arenas do not), the promoter is also charged for Seat Construction. Check with the facility manager to find out how much it costs, and add 15 percent.

Most facilities that present concerts on a regular basis have spotlights. Nevertheless, they usually charge a Spotlight Rental Fee of $50 or $75 per spotlight per night. This figure does not include the spotlight operator's fee. Normally, I've used between four and six spotlights for theater shows. In arenas, I've used as many as twelve.

The Fork Lift saves a lot of time and manpower in unloading heavy equipment from the headliner's trucks, transporting it, and raising it onto the stage. Some halls give the fork lift to the promoter gratuitously. Others charge you a Fork Lift Rental fee.

Scaffolding, the building material for portable stages, towers, and audio mix platforms, is usually rented to the promoter by the facility. Working from the headliner's stage blueprint, which is usually contained in the concert rider, the head of the stagehands should be able to quote a realistic estimate of scaffolding costs.

Some attractions require images of themselves to be projected on the sports arena's overhead television screens. There is an additional Projector charge for this. Other attractions use films or TV projection equipment onstage as part of their act. Projectors are either rented locally, from audiovisual supply houses, or furnished by the headliner. Find out, in the latter case, whether they are included in the headliner's talent fee.

An additional expense item, overlooked by many start-up concert promoters, is the cost of renting long extension cords, or Cables, used to connect sound and lighting equipment to the facility's power outlets. Early access to the facility's electrical power supply, so as not to delay set-up time, is absolutely essential. A preliminary meeting or phone conversation with the facility's chief electrician is highly recommended.

Sound is the elaborate sound system used for the presentation of rock concerts. Lights, which should not be confused with the house lights and spotlights, are the stage lights above the attraction. The cost of Sound and Lights has risen dramatically in recent years. For major headliners, who carry their own sound and lights with them, it's another case of take it or leave it, unilateral negotiating power. The promoter must pay whatever price the headliner has established for renting his equipment, or forfeit a confirmed concert. There's simply no room in today's business for promoters to negotiate this major expense with superstars.

In defense of the attraction, I don't think that most superstars travel with their own sound and light equipment because they're trying to rip off the concert promoter. The superstar considers his sound and light equipment an extension of his music. The agency is offering a total package to the promoter—music, sound, and lights—and all three ingredients must be perfectly meshed. The best way to insure this balance is to have the attraction rehearse with sound and lights for several weeks prior to hitting the road, and to have the sound and lights accompany the attraction from city to city. Most headliners, in fact, will postpone an engagement rather than perform without their own sound and lights. They will not take a chance on playing with unfamiliar equipment.

Promoters can be assured, if they're paying top dollar for leased equipment from a superstar, that it's the best equipment in the world and that it's working perfectly. When they're playing in front of 20,000 screaming teenagers, acts can't afford to use less than state-of-the-art equipment. The only variable left to discuss with the attraction's road manager concerning sound and lights is how many amplifiers and speakers are needed. A 10,000-seater may not require as many amplifiers and speakers as an outdoor 60,000-seater. Speak with the agency, or the attraction's road manager, and try to agree on a price for a specific number of amplifiers and speakers for the hall.

Support attractions and opening acts may also travel with their own sound and lights. In cases where the promoter is contractually obligated to furnish sound and lights, the promoter must consult the artist's concert rider for directions and specifications. The facility manager or booking agency will be able to advise start-up concert promoters which suppliers in town offer properly maintained equipment and dependable service.

The last item under Production—Curtains and Backdrop—is for curtains used to prevent audiences from looking into the wings of a theater, or for backdrops that prevent audiences from seeing the bare walls of the facility. Most facilities charge promoters a rental fee for Curtains and Backdrop.

Production Personnel covers the labor force responsible for everything that happens onstage or behind stage. Stagehands are the men who physically put the show on. Their job is to build the stage, construct the seats, unload trucks with their fork lifts, take that equipment and place it onstage, move the equipment during set changes, and return the equipment to the trucks at the completion of the show. Stagehands usually belong to a stagehands union. They are autonomous from the facility, the attraction, the agency, and the promoter. Their fees, in my experience, run anywhere from $5,000 to $15,000 per arena show, sometimes more. They can be very, very expensive, especially if your concert goes overtime.

Electricians, also unionized, handle the electrical installations for the facility. They should also be consulted prior to the event for an outside estimate (plus 15 percent) of how much time and labor they will require to do their job.

Spotlight Operators are usually part of the stagehand's union. Their actual cost is easier to ascertain than the actual cost of the other stagehands. Check the rider to see how many spotlights are required, then speak with the head of the stagehands union to see how many spotlight operators are required in the union facility to do the job.

The next three listings are for people who may be employed by the promoter. Since I am not a technically oriented concert promoter, I've always had a Production Coordinator to assist me. His job is to advise me whether certain types of production work, recommended by the stagehands or the electricians, need to be done. He also coordinates various elements of the concert for me, between the front end (box office) and the tail end (backstage) of the concert.

The Stage Manager, the promoter's Man Friday onstage, is available to answer any questions, smooth any ruffled feathers, and assist in any way toward completing the concert set-up prior to the headliner's scheduled sound check. The Assistant Stage Manager takes direction from the stage manager. Depending on the size of the concert, the promoter may need each of these three employees, or just two, or one.

The Teamsters union may have a contract with the facility that calls for the Teamsters, not the stagehands, to unload the equipment from the trucks. Check with the facility manager, or chief of stagehands, to see if the facility has such a contract with the Teamsters. If it does, you will have to include a Teamsters expense on the PCA form. Contact the local Teamsters office for their hourly rates.

Rider listings, taken from the headliner's concert rider and the support attraction's concert rider, will enable the promoter to budget the additional expense items covered by these contract addenda. Limousines are the luxury rented vehicles that will pick up the attraction at the airport, take the attraction to the hotel, deliver the attraction to the facility for a sound check, return the attraction to the hotel, take the attraction back to the facility for the evening's performance, and return the attraction to the hotel and, eventually, the airport.

Major attractions normally require two or three limousines per concert. Their cost is roughly $200 each. The best way to keep costs down on limousine rentals is to reach an accord with the attraction that the promoter will only pay for concert-related use of the limousines. If the attraction wishes to drive around until 5:00 in the morning, and the concert was over at 11:30 the night before, the attraction should pay the bill between 11:30 and 5:00. I have instructed limousine companies that I will not be responsible for billing beyond the completion of the concert. Still, if the attraction wants to be nasty, and you're told to pay the entire bill, you have no choice but to ante up the loot.

The Piano is whatever brand of concert grand that is required for the engagement. The attraction will tell you whether they need a six-foot, seven-foot, or nine-foot piano. A number of attractions are beginning to carry their own pianos, but normally the piano is rented by the promoter from the local dealer who sells that particular brand of piano.

Most headliners and support attractions travel with their own electronic Organs, but may require the promoter to pay a rental fee for their use. Tuners are the people that tune the piano and organs prior to the start of the concert. The rider may also require these instruments to be tuned during the intermission of the concert. Most facilities use house tuners who charge predictable rates.

Refreshments covers the catering of meals backstage for the attraction, and breakfast, lunch, and dinner for the attraction's production crew. This does not include the union stagehands, but even so you're talking today about expenses that range from $500 to $1,500 per show. Detailed menus are included in the concert rider.

The Hostess, an employee of the promoter, may be assigned to supervise the catering of meals and oversee the correct purchase of spirits and the chilling of those spirits.

Besides renting limousines for the attraction, the promoter is often asked to rent a Truck or Van to carry the attraction's luggage and costumes, and the traveling crew's luggage. This is a necessary expense: I've known production crews to exceed twenty people.

Trailers, or motor homes, are required for outdoor festivals. The trailer is used as the dressing room and office for the attraction and the attraction's personal manager. These are predictable, rentable items.

Cranes may also be required for outdoor festivals if you have to "fly" a sound system, or lift an entire stage.

Attractions usually ask for a Telephone to be installed in their dressing room. The promoter will have to pay for installation of the telephone, and all the calls that are made on that phone. I'm pleased to say that I've never had the unpleasantness of being charged with long distance telephone calls made from this phone by an attraction. They have either reversed charges or used their credit card numbers to make the calls. This has been one of the least expensive and most predictable rider requests I've had to honor.

Insurance, another major expense often overlooked by the start-up promoter, is your protection against extensive liability. Most concert facilities already have minimum fire, property, and damage insurance. But as the risk to the facility goes up—and 20,000 people at a rock concert increases the risk substantially—the facility is going to insist that the promoter take out additional insurance covering that concert. Without proof that the concert is adequately insured, most facilities will not allow an engagement to go on.

Personal Liability coverage is the facility's chief concern. Premiums range from $300,000 coverage per disaster and $100,000 per person affected in that disaster, to $1,000,000 coverage per disaster and $300,000 per person affected in that disaster, to $3,000,000 coverage per disaster and $1,000,000 per person affected in that disaster. In a major facility, such as Madison Square Garden, the price of this premium may be as high as $5,000 for a single event. Property Damage covers any property that is lost, stolen, or destroyed at the facility by one or more of the paying customers. Property damage insurance is usually for a much smaller figure than personal liability insurance.

Fire insurance and Building Damage insurance protect the facility in case of fire or damage to the facility. Stick-up insurance offers protection to the promoter if the box office is robbed.

Other types of insurance protection may be thrust upon the promoter by the agent. It may be necessary to insure the attraction's equipment, or the attraction itself. For each of these different types of insurance, the promoter must ascertain whether he is obligated to buy the coverage; how much the coverage should be; when the coverage should begin; and how long the coverage should last. Most reputable insurance brokers will be able to obtain this coverage for the promoter from an insurance specialist in rock concerts. As always, when you're starting up or doing a one-shot concert, your bargaining position is disproportionate to the supplier of goods or services. If you were able to guarantee the insurance salesman that you were doing one hundred concerts each year, and that they were all going to be insured, the unit price of insurance would drop. But for one concert, it is necessary to grin and bear it. You must pay the quotation price, period.

Legal and Accounting covers any special work the promoter's attorney or accountant may have to do in terms of reviewing contracts and riders, negotiating with city agencies (i.e., the parks department, municipal employees union), and issuing financial statements to the attraction, agency, or investors. These are isolated special payments, and should not be confused with what the promoter pays his lawyer or accountant as a monthly retainer for routine professional services.

ASCAP, BMI, and SESAC are the three U.S. societies that license and collect performing rights fees for composers and publishers of copyrighted music. The composer or composers of music in each attraction are affiliated with at least one of these performing rights societies. The societies charge concert promoters a fee for the right to perform the composer's music publicly where admission fees (ticket sales) are involved.

Performing rights fees for concerts are relatively small. They range from $50 per show to $300 per show per society, depending on the size of the facility. To find out whether you're obligated to pay one, two, or three performing rights licensing fees, ask the attraction's agent which songs are scheduled to be performed during the engagement, and whether these songs are licensed through ASCAP, BMI, or SESAC. If the songs are licensed through one society exclusively, the promoter need pay only that society. However, if half of the songs, for example, are licensed through ASCAP, and half are licensed through SESAC, the promoter will have to pay two licensing fees. For further information contact ASCAP, BMI, and SESAC directly.

Promoter's Direct Concert Expenses and Production Coordinator's Direct Concert Expenses are used to budget such personal items as airplane tickets (Transportation), if it's an out-of-town concert; living accommodations and meals (Hotel), also if it's an out-of-town concert; and Other costs incurred by the promoter or production coordinator, such as cab fare, writing pads, and pocket calculators (absolutely essential in this business).

Advertising and Promotion covers the cost of telling the public what you're doing. Briefly, the items that may be involved in a typical concert ad/PR campaign include Radio (commercials), Television (commercials), Publications (newspaper and magazine ads), PR (Public Relations, designed to get coverage of the event through newspaper stories and TV and radio interviews), and Production (the cost of producing commercials, press kits, and newspaper ads). The cost of placing ads in the media mix of radio, TV, and newsprint, plus a fee for professional public relations help, can easily exceed $15,000 for a major concert.

Other advertising expenses include the printing of Signs, Posters, and Flyers, and the changing of the theater's Marquee (large sign) to announce your show. All advertising costs are predictable. Publicity costs are less predictable, but you may be able to establish a ceiling with the publicity agent. A thorough analysis of advertising and public relations is saved for a later chapter of this book (chapter 11).

First Aid covers accidents that occur to the promoter's audience. Somebody gets a leg twisted, or an arm broken, because of a crowd squeeze. Somebody gets paranoid because of the drug he or she took. Somebody gets into a fight and needs medical attention. The promoter may be required, either by the attraction or the facility, to have a certain number of Doctors, Nurses, and Ambulances available during the concert. Check with the facility manager for rates and listings of medical services.

Overtime, the bane of all concert promoters, covers time-and-a-half or double-time payments to the facility's stagehands if they are unable to restore the facility to its normal operating condition within their regular work shift. To ascertain whether you will be hit with overtime payments, ask when the stagehands' regular shift ends and overtime begins. Then contact the attraction's agent and double check when the show is scheduled to be over. Check back with the head of the stagehands and see whether you have enough stagehands to get the job done. The concert rider blueprints, plus some guidance from the attraction's road manager, should help the promoter gauge properly whether he should budget an Overtime expense and, if so, how much.

Sunday Premiums, another type of production penalty, are the additional costs promoters are charged by various unions for staging concerts on Sunday. Contact the head of each of the unions—box office, stagehands, electricians, Teamsters, and so on—for further information.

Gratuities are tips the promoter may wish to bestow on a backstage guard, bouncer, gofer, or some other person who deserves some ready cash. I've budgeted anywhere from $100 to $500 for gratuities, depending on the size of the concert.

All conceivable production costs have now been accounted for. By adding them up, the promoter will know his Total Costs. Audience Break-Even is a figure reached by dividing the average ticket price into Total Costs. This is an approximate figure, since it involves average ticket prices rather than actual ticket prices, but it does provide the promoter with a yardstick for determining how many bodies are needed just to break even.

The Actual Gross Less Taxes is the total amount of money the concert has generated through ticket sales, less applicable taxes. By subtracting Total Costs from Actual Gross Less Taxes, the promoter will arrive at the Gross Profit figure. Don't be surprised if your Gross Profit has to be expressed in negative (loss) parentheses.

If you've gotten through this cursory analysis of production costs in one sitting, congratulations. I know it's not the most interesting reading. It doesn't have the built-in excitement of negotiating with major agencies for name talent, or actually producing the show. But here is what the promoter's career comes down to. This is the bottom line, where you either stay in business or go broke. In presenting, for the first time in book form, the totality of production costs and possible cost overruns, I wonder whether I have begun to discourage any readers about the likelihood of building a career as a concert promoter.

You should feel apprehensive. The financial obligations of a promoter aren't finished when he knows how much his talent and facility are going to cost. They've just begun. There are other general overhead costs the promoter will encounter by the time he starts promoting regular shows with major talent—such as office rent, telephone, full-time secretary, office equipment, payroll taxes, postage, legal and accounting retainers, transportation, entertainment, printing, and insurance. If you think it's difficult to walk away from the end of a year with a $50,000 salary for yourself, you're right. Without major attractions, without access to the best facilities in town, the chances of being a true financial success—of actually being able to bank $50,000 a year—are nil. That, unfortunately, is reality.

The PCA form, besides showing the potential promoter the full scope of his likely financial obligations, also gives an excellent idea of the promoter's responsibilities. Timing is the critical issue here. I urge new concert promoters, when they begin discussing possible concerts with agents, to get into the habit of filling in their PCA forms before the deal is signed. Know where you stand. It can be quite painful, but you will discover that so many of the concerts that seemed to be such good deals for you will give the attraction exposure, provide income for the artist and the agency, but generate little or no income for the promoter.

Remember that in writing this book I am principally concerned that aspiring promoters realize the truthful conditions of being in this business. How much work is involved, and how minimal the profit potential can be! It is already incredibly expensive to promote concerts, and prices will continue to climb. It is up to the individual to decide whether the means justify the end. You can call yourself a promoter—you can even appear to be a successful promoter, with major headliners bringing in solid audiences. But if you don't sell out, you may lose your profit. Even if you do sell out, your total production costs may completely erase your profit and give you a significant loss for the evening.

Without something very special going for you, such as a monopoly over the leading rock showcase in town, I doubt whether any start-up promoter in today's business can make enough money to be considered financially successful. Some promoters are less concerned than others about bottom line imperatives, but if you are interested in making money as a concert promoter, I'd suggest that you come to grips with the realities of this PCA form as soon as possible.

6

The Facility

ACCESS TO THE RIGHT FACILITY or facilities in your town can make a world of difference in attempting to become an active concert promoter. Securing a hall may not require as much finesse as getting talent, but if you can't get the hall, you won't get the attraction. This chapter discusses the different types of facilities that exist, how to obtain them, and what to expect in a facility contract.

Because of the developmental service nature of this business, with concert promoters constantly being asked by agents to showcase their new artists, the ideal facility configuration has the promoter involved in not one, but preferably three prime showcases. Clubs, the smallest venues, are for start-up artists. Concert halls or their equivalent—college and high school auditoriums, local Y's, churches, carnivals, and tennis clubs—are for middle-level artists. Sports arenas, race tracks, outdoor stadiums, and summer festivals are for major attractions and superstars. Occasionally, a superstar may want to return to his club beginnings, or a start-up attraction will get the nod to open for a major act in a 20,000-seater, but generally artists at the start-up, middle-level, and superstar rank will perform only in venues whose stature parallels their own.

It is very important for concert promoters to start working with developing acts at either the club or concert hall level. This is where the promoter pays his dues to the act and the agency: if it's a good marriage between the promoter and the act, and the promoter has political clout with the major facility in his town, it will be impossible for an outside promoter to come in and subsequently steal the act.

Virtually every major U.S. concert promoter has structured himself to handle acts through this tiered facility approach. Bill Graham developed his acts at the Fillmore East and West before presenting them in major arenas. I had the Academy of Music in New York City for developmental purposes, and later I promoted the acts that survived at Madison Square Garden, the Orange Bowl, Shea Stadium, and other major venues. Ron Delsener, who has a very favorable relationship with Madison Square Garden and the Nassau Coliseum on Long Island, uses a summer concert series in Central Park and the Palladium (which used to be the Academy of Music) to bring acts along. Larry Magid, one of the most powerful U.S. promoters, has the Philadelphia market covered at all three levels: the start-up attractions perform at his Bijou Cafe; the middle-level acts play the Tower Theater; and the superstars are presented at the Spectrum or John F. Kennedy Stadium, which seats 100,000 people.

Building up a two- or three-layered facility operation may take years of arduous work for the start-up promoter, and may require that he set up business in a city or town slightly off the beaten path. But it is essential to be in both the developmental and assured sellout ends of the industry at all times, if you want to make concert promotion a permanent career.

Just as new attractions use clubs as the crucible for getting kinks out of their show, so should the start-up promoter look first to club experiences for professional seasoning. Lack of funding to go out and buy a club should not be a deterrent to the determined potential promoter. Jobs are available as the talent buyer for a club, or the person in charge of amateur-night showcases. Once you are inside the door, opportunities to meet people, impress them with your talents, and move onto the next career step should present themselves in fairly rapid succession. The best way to obtain one of these point-of-entry positions, if you don't have an uncle in the business as I did, is to make friends with the present talent buyer, discover when that person is planning to move on (the turnover is tremendous—these jobs pay next to nothing), and offer your services to the club owner. If the timing is right, and you appear to have something on the ball, the job should be yours.

From here on, it's performance that counts. You have to be better than your competition. You have to convince people that they can rely upon you to do whatever they ask, and that you're totally honest. Any halfway decent club in the United States is going to see its fair share of promising new attractions, agents, and other elements of the rock and roll industry. The ultimate test of whether you'll be trusted to assume larger responsibilities as a developing promoter is not a function of how well you study production technique. It's a function of *you*: your attitudes, your personality, your behavior, your looks. Unfortunately, I can't do much more than inform you of this reality in terms of improving your chances for success.

Having studied the mechanics of concert promotion at a club, and having won at least the tacit approval of an important booking agency, the start-up promoter will be able to present his first concert hall productions. This step is very critical: it is the equivalent of a coming-out party for the promoter, with every fault, every mistake, deducted from the promoter's scorecard with the industry. If the mistakes are tolerable, and the promoter is able to keep his head above water financially, the relationship between the agency and the promoter will be cemented.

The approach to the manager of the facility should be very straightforward: you, the promoter, having presented a number of acts at the club where you work (your track record), would be interested in establishing a relationship with the facility. To prove your worth, you would like the opportunity to present [the attraction]. Then give the facility manager a copy of the act's current press kit, which will have been prepared by the artist's record company. Briefly you'll describe the attraction to the facility manager, telling him where they've played recently, the reception they've received, and the type of audience the attraction appeals to. If the trial concert works out well, you conclude, you would welcome an opportunity to present more concerts at that facility. If you're able to leave a deposit with the hall, and the act has a clean reputation, you should have no problems.

If it's your first concert hall show, try to do it at a facility that includes essential services, such as box office, ushers, stagehands, and maintenance people, as part of the rental package. Don't overload yourself with added logistical responsibilities. Devote your time to the more important things: servicing the act, producing an excellent concert, and settling the finances to everyone's mutual satisfaction (including, you hope, your own).

After several years of continued activity, during which the promoter's abilities and will to survive are tested beyond imagination, the promoter stands on the brink of something happening. The object you've been pushing toward, the major concert facility in town, may now regard you as a legitimate, veteran concert promoter who can be trusted with a 15,000-seat plus venue. If it is an open facility without a quasi-monopolistic exclusivity involving one promoter, you should be able to take your shot at the big leagues. But in most cases today, the major facilities in the largest U.S. metropolitan centers will be off limits to outside independent promoters. Here's why:

Fifteen years ago, when large-scale rock concerts were just beginning to be contemplated, facility managers realized that they needed rock and roll experts to advise them about which acts to showcase, and how to reach this potential new audience of fans. Quite a few of the major facilities, after seeing what damages could be inflicted on their halls by errant adolescents, decided to go the safe route: henceforth they would work with only one promoter, the best promoter they could find locally, and make it incumbent on this promoter not only to service the attraction and the agency, but also the facility.

Fifteen years later, promoters like Bill Graham, the Belkin Brothers in Cleveland, and Larry Magid are still in complete command of their facilities' rock concert program. These professionals know what they're doing, and the main thing they do, as far as the owners of the facilities are concerned, is generate an enormous amount of income—much more, in fact, than most facilities collect annually for sporting events.

Quasi-monopolistic relationships may be illegal, but in the absence of very expensive antitrust litigation—far beyond the reach of promoters acting as individuals—they will persist. The choices left to the start-up promoters of the 1980s are few. Possibly they can work out an arrangement whereby they will cosponsor a show at the facility with the entrenched promoter (this usually involves payment of a service fee of $2,500 or more for menial work, or 5 percent of the concert's actual gross, less taxes, for more substantial participation). The more likely alternatives are for the start-up promoter either to move on to an open city, or to try and establish his own quasi-monopolistic fiefdom in some smaller U.S. town. Neither of these paths, unfortunately, can be branded an original idea.

Some of the newer approaches to getting control of an important facility coincide with the development of new directions in music. Disco music, which has taken phenomenal jumps in popularity since its development several years ago, may also mandate a specialized environment, as well as the necessary excuse, for a latter-day disco expert to take control of an attractive venue. It's impossible for me to go beyond suggesting the importance of being original, and pointing up the added risk one takes in trying to develop a more specialized market. What might work for Detroit could be anathema in Nashville or Atlanta. Concert-buying habits among fifteen-year-old San Francisco girls are probably slightly different from concert-buying habits for fifteen-year-old girls in Boston. The promoters who can figure out riddles such as these (no one else will do it for you) deserve to go places in the industry.

Prior to contract, the facility will be asked by the promoter to hold dates for a potential concert. It's absolutely not customary to leave a deposit for holding a date. If you have a reasonable working relationship with the facility manager's office, they are more than likely to agree to hold the date until some specific time in the near future, or they will hold the date in general. If someone else comes in with a firm offer for that date, the facility should call and say, "We will give you twenty-four hours to give us a firm acceptance. Then, since we're turning down another event, we will expect a deposit from you."

Hall fees, like talent costs, are not negotiable. Halls either charge a flat fee, payable in installments (deposit plus balance withheld by the facility at the conclusion of the concert), or they charge a percentage of gross receipts, between 12 and 22.5 percent less applicable taxes, against the guaranteed rental fee. For example, a hall may offer the promoter a 15 percent percentage against guarantee deal. The guarantee is for $3,000, but the concert grosses $25,000 after taxes, so the hall will take 15 percent of the gate, or

$3,750. The deal is for either one or the other: the guarantee or the percentage.

Sometimes, however, facilities will ask for a guarantee plus a percentage in excess of a certain break figure. In the sample facility contract shown in appendix C, the hall requested a guaranteed rental fee of $27,500, payable in installments; an additional $27,500 for estimated personnel, services, equipment, and materials costs for the concert; and 22.5 percent of the net gate receipts beyond $130,000. If, for example, the concert grossed $135,000, the hall would have taken another $1,125 (22.5 percent of $5,000) from its box-office receipts for that concert. Halls never get cheated out of overage money. In fact, halls never get cheated out of any money: their policy is to withhold the difference between actual costs and estimated costs from the net concert receipts they ultimately pass on to the promoter.

This is one of the reasons why it is so important to know what services the facility intends to provide, what insurance and security requirements the facility wishes to make, and how many seats are actually available for the concert. The PCA form should be extremely helpful to start-up promoters in determining the gamut of production costs they are likely to incur. A detailed facility contract is another excellent guidepost for the promoter. It tells the promoter what he can and cannot do. It provides a chronology for the move-in, rehearsal, performance, and move-out of the artist's show. It gives the promoter deadlines for submitting deposits and certifications that the concert is adequately insured. It is a valuable document to be read and reread, so that problem areas can be identified and resolved with the facility in advance of their actual occurrence.

Facility contracts, no matter how many pages they are and how obtuse their legal terminology gets to be, boil down to elementary issues of supply and demand. If you, the promoter, wish to develop a continuing relationship with the facility, you will have to abide by whatever the facility tells you to do. There is very little room for negotiation. There is even less room for shoddy professionalism during the actual performance. It is imperative to honor the terms and spirit of the contract; otherwise, there will be no tomorrow for the promoter at that facility.

The best way for the reader to familiarize himself with a facility contract is to read the sample license agreement in its entirety. It is one of the most comprehensive facility contracts I have ever dealt with. It goes beyond being merely a four-wall contract in the following ways:

a. it limits the promoter's source of income to net gate receipts from ticket sales; the promoter has no share in the facility's concession income on programs, souvenirs, food, and drink;

b. it requires the promoter to submit for approval copies of proposed advertisements using the facility name;

c. it requires the promoter to indemnify the facility from any claims whatsoever, including court costs and attorney fees, against the promoter in connection with the promoter's event;

d. it requires the promoter to take out policies for public liability, property damage, fire/legal/liability, workmen's compensation, and employers liability insurance from an A-rated insurance company (or better) at least thirty days prior to the event; the promoter will also have to insure his own employees and himself, if he hasn't already;

e. it requires the promoter to contract all musicians, other than the attraction's self-contained unit, through the facility;

f. it requires the promoter to pay the facility $5,000 for each performance during which a member of the attraction encourages members of the audience to leave their seats;

g. it requires the promoter to reimburse the facility for any fees paid to ASCAP, BMI, and SESAC;

h. it reserves for the facility itself the right to deploy photographers, camera crews, and the press as it sees fit;

i. it requires the promoter to declare in writing his policy on who should be permitted backstage before, during, and after the concert; the promoter must also prepare suitable identification badges for guests, workers, and members of the press to be admitted backstage.

Such attention to detail, coupled with the physical dimensions of certain facilities, suggests the reality of being able to promote concerts at major venues. The facility won't admit raw amateurs: an apprenticeship with smaller concert halls and clubs is not only desirable, in terms of developing new talent, but necessary in order to impress a facility manager with the promoter's qualifications for using his major facility. Fortunately, it is much easier to gain admittance to smaller venues, such as concert halls and clubs, than to outsized venues. Most halls that are not being used 365 days a year, in my experience, are eager to make the acquaintance of bright, financially solvent concert promoters who can furnish them the means for boosting their annual revenues. Finding these smaller facilities, along with developing relationships with important booking agents, offers the greatest probability for one day being able to present attractions at major venues.

In the next chapter I'll go beyond this rational approach and suggest ways for coping with perhaps the greatest problem faced by most potential concert promoters: their inability to find a start-up job in the concert promotion industry.

7

How to Get into the Business

IT SEEMS that there are more and more young people who want to be able to dress casually; who want to be able to work on a non–9:00 to 5:00 basis; who want to do something that they consider culturally pertinent. Many of these young people may decide on concert promotion as their first choice for a potential career.

There are no fluent answers for the question of how to get into the promotion business. It is one of the most difficult, maddening industries to break into, especially if you're totally unconnected with the major agencies. But it can be done. If you have not been intimidated by all the horrors I've painted about this business—if you really want to promote concerts—if you're prepared to make a lot of sacrifices, and you have some entrepreneural talent—then this chapter recommending different ways to get into the business should be helpful.

Access to the major agencies is the key to becoming a major concert promoter, along with cultivating a prime facility for developing talent. Money by itself won't do it, and neither, despite the manner in which this industry is sometimes portrayed, will sexual overtures—it's business, first and foremost. If you want to become a concert promoter, and you're totally on the outside, you must be prepared to face facts. You mean absolutely nothing to the agency. The agency doesn't need you, and probably doesn't even want you.

Even if you're on the inside—if you've promoted circuses or family shows for twenty years, or you have an excellent reputation as a publisher or record company person—your experience may not get you a rock concert in today's business. It is essential to be realistic about how people get started in the concert promotion industry today. It's not because of favors. It's not because one person has more money than another person. It's knowing how to service the agency. It's being able to show the agency that the business plan you've developed for promoting their new attractions is better than your competitor's business plan.

I've already discussed the territorial control that major promoters have achieved in many strategic U.S. cities through either overt or covert quasi monopolies with major concert facilities. These monopolies are maintained not only by keeping the facility owner happy, but through very personal, political relationships with agents and managers. In many cases these relationships are almost impossible to break. The bond between agent and promoter goes deeper than friendship and proven honesty: it is based on the fact that the major concert promoter can be relied upon to do a professional show. Agents don't need the headache of worrying about whether their new start-up promoter can handle the assignment. They take the conservative approach—they go with the pros.

Undercutting established promoters by offering to pay larger talent fees is not the way to break into the business. Very often, when numbers get thrown around, the "winner" turns out to be the loser. The promoter who pays the higher price for the attraction will more than likely have overpaid. Besides, major agencies aren't usually persuaded by the lure of short-term windfall profits. It's more important to build a long-term track record of consistently solid promotions, of good performances, of turnaway shows. Some attractions, in fact, purposely hold back on their price. They want promoters to be able to afford them. They want promoters to think that they're getting a bargain, so that they'll work harder at selling out and making a profit. But always, the attraction and the agency are looking for experienced promoters. They won't sell to a start up promoter unless the act itself is new.

Having discussed these negative features, I must reiterate that there are opportunities for careers in the concert promotion business. There are still towns and facilities in the United States that are either completely or partially open, and that are approachable by start-up promoters. Regardless of the approach you take—and I'm going to mention eight different approaches that I know have worked for some of the most successful contemporary concert promoters—you'll discover that, in order to get ahead, you must be patient, patient, patient.

1. Secondary City Approach.   If you want to enter the concert promotion business as a mainstream major rock promoter without spending a long apprenticeship elsewhere, look to the secondary U.S. cities that don't have steady promoters—cities that are free of monopolies and entrenched relationships with agents and managers.

I can think of several examples of how this approach has proven successful in the past. Concerts East, a Long Island–based promotion company, used to have three principal promoters: Phil Buzeo, the owner, Tony Ruffino, and Larry Vaughn. Stiff competition for the Nassau Coliseum existed between Concerts East and Ron Delsener, the major

New York City promoter. That problem, probably compounded by internal disputes among Buzeo, Ruffino, and Vaughn, made it necessary for Ruffino and Vaughn to find other markets in which to promote concerts. They discovered that Birmingham, Alabama, was a wide-open market, and that it had the necessary facilities. Ruffino and Vaughn relocated to Birmingham. They're now comfortable major promoters, unchallenged in Birmingham, with the experience and professionalism to make them hard to displace.

The Belkin Brothers, who are so strong in Cleveland, noticed that nobody seemed to be controlling Cincinnati. Today the Belkin Brothers have an exclusivity on the largest concert hall in that city.

Alex Cooley, a Washington, D.C., promoter, noticed that things were wavering in the Miami, Florida, market after my departure. Cooley went down to Miami, made the necessary arrangements with local facility managers, and established himself as a major Miami concert promoter.

There are secondary cities all over the United States that have no major promoters. Some cities in Virginia which do really good business have yet to be locked up. Texas has always been fumbling for a major promoter who will dominate the entire state. These opportunities should be given close inspection by any person interested in promoting major attractions. They are not opportunities for the raw beginner, but they do represent the fastest way for moving into the big leagues.

2. *Suburban Approach.* Suburbia, where the greatest share of per capita income resides, where people go to shop for records, blue jeans, and sneakers, is a major growth market for rock concert promotions. My own career as a promoter started as co-owner of the Capitol Theater in Portchester, New York, the first suburban rock concert emporium in America.

Any high-density suburban area that has a large concert facility and no exclusive concert promoter will do. You may have to spend a lot of time researching different potential suburban communities for their reaction to rock music. Some will like it, others won't permit it.

Convincing arguments can be made for agency support of suburban concerts. It may be more convenient for young people to attend a suburban concert than to drive into the city. Commuting costs and meals may also be less in Suburbia—an important consideration for money-conscious teenagers. Parents may feel better about sending their children to a suburban concert than to the neighboring city, with its usually higher crime rate. These factors, coupled with the obvious demographic makeup of middle- and upper-middle-class Suburbia, may tip the scales in favor of the potential promoter with access to the suburban concert hall.

3. Working for an Established Promoter. Realistically, the complete outsider is not going to be able to establish himself in a secondary city or a suburban rock theater without working for somebody else first. A good job in a well-connected music company—preferably a concert organization—is the best shortcut to any successful career as a promoter. But how do you get a job with the top promoter in town?

Here is one situation where it doesn't pay to come on too strong. The last thing a successful concert promoter wants to do is train an ultimate competitor. When I took on employees, it was important for me to feel that these were people who were ambitious and helpful, but not people who wanted someday to own my business. If you're able to meet the top promoter in town, don't say to him, "I want to be a promoter." Ask instead for a job as a production assistant, stage manager, or gofer. Tell the promoter that you're a good typist, or that you take shorthand, or that you possess other practical skills, that you're willing to work at a very reasonable hourly wage (less than an employment agency charges), on or off the books (off the books can save the promoter lots of money).

Tell the promoter that your hours are flexible, and that the reason you're willing to work for less is your fascination with music or the rock and roll culture, not your desire to promote concerts. Make it sound as good as you can, and for heaven's sake look sincere. If you're young, and you really can be useful, sooner or later a job will open up. There is a huge turnover rate for production underlings, primarily because the pay is bad and the hours are long.

If you do not get a job with a promoter, make sure you stick with it. Be fantastic. Make the promoter realize how valuable you are to his organization. Let the promoter offer to expose you to other areas of the business. It's important to know your place, but once inside the environment it's almost impossible not to learn what it's really like to promote a concert, and to make invaluable connections.

4. Record Company Approach. If you can't get a job with a concert promotion company, your next best bet would be to work for a record company. Some record companies actually have their own concert promotion departments, since virtually every new album released today coincides with the start of an artist's cross-country or world concert tour. By monitoring live concert attendance figures, the record company can determine whether they have a potential hit album on their hands, and where to spend their advertising dollars.

The record company's in-house concert promotion department may be part of the artist development, artist relations, or product management divisions. It may simply be called the tour support department, since this is the functional phrase used to describe what record companies actually do in the concert area, other than accumulate marketing data: finance new equipment and transportation vehicles for the attraction; subsidize cooperative newspaper, radio, or television ads (the promoter pays half, the record company pays half); and occasionally guarantee the promoter against any financial losses (i.e., short-fall insurance) in showcasing the record company's new, unknown artists. Short-fall insurance is a prevalent feature in the European concert promotion business.

5. *Facility Approach.*   Another way to make contact with the all-important agency heads is through an apprenticeship at a major concert facility, where you'll gain valuable on-line experience working with the various unions and promoters, and coping with eleventh-hour crises. Rather than being a participant, you can watch start-up promoters make mistakes from the sidelines.

6. *Trend Approach.*   A different, less direct approach for entering the concert promotion business is by capitalizing on a new musical trend. Major promoters, by virtue of their success, are limited to dealing with the biggest attractions, the biggest arenas, the biggest agencies and managers. The next important musical trend may be happening right under their noses, but they may no longer have the time or interest to react to it.

Right now in New York City, a club called CBGB's is doing very will with new wave music. The owners of CBGB's felt that new wave was starting to happen, and began sponsoring more and more new wave bands in their small club. Then they decided to become the major promoter of new wave in New York City. After a relatively short period of time, their club showcases generated enough capital for CBGB's to take over the 2,000-seat Second Avenue Theater. Now, in addition to its successful club, CBGB's has a much larger venue for new wave concerts, and the market is growing.

Don Freedman, a successful promoter of jazz, saw that jazz record sales were picking up. Freedman made an arrangement with WRVR-FM, the leading jazz station in New York City, to cosponsor a special series of jazz concerts. The results have been very satisfying for Freedman, WRVR, and the record companies whose artists were involved.

Disco, rhythm and blues, reggae, calypso—opportunities are always beckoning on the "new trend" front. If you're into the music, and you're patient, this might be an even better approach than working for a concert promoter or record company.

7. *Artist Approach.*   If you're not able to hook up with a leading agency, but you're anxious to get into the promotion swing, you can develop a direct relationship with a start-up artist. The relationship can either be promoter to artist or manager/promoter to artist. This raises the question of whether it is advisable to wear more than one hat in the music business. Personally, I think that it's too risky for a start-up promoter to be a manager or record producer as well. Promoting concerts is a very time-consuming, emotion-draining business that demands a high level of expertise. You can only become the expert by devoting full time to one thing, at least when you're starting out and you don't have a staff.

If you want to be a publisher in addition to being a promoter (and this wouldn't be fair unless you've actually made some contribution to the artist's music), that's more manageable. Have the artist sign a publishing contract with you, and then subcontract with an established music publishing company for administration. But if you want to be a personal manager in addition to being a concert promoter, you have to make a decision. Which would you rather be, a manager or a promoter? Each is a full-time job, and you can't be in two places at once. It's better for start-up promoters to think monothematically. Do one thing at a time, because that's probably the only way to do it right.

8. Club Approach.   The last approach may be the best one. Instead of going for concerts, you shoot for a jazz club, or a trend club, or a record company–subsidized showcase club, such as The Bottom Line in New York City or the Roxy in Los Angeles. Here you're dealing with something tangible. You own the facility, or at least you control it. You sell whiskey and food. You're working with small acts that aren't overwhelming you with demands or extravagant production requests.

It's a relatively good situation to be in. You're offering valuable development service to the agents and managers. You're not constantly begging for superstars. You're giving the agency's new attractions a chance to work. It's a marvelous way to meet agents, to meet new attractions early in their careers. Then, when you're ready, you can exploit your club relationships. You can talk to the agency about playing acts in concerts. The agency will have done business with you and learned your value to them. It's a marvelous approach. And I'm sure that there are still many cities in the United States that would appreciate an intimate, Bottom Line–type club.

For each of these cases, I've described how to get into the business so that eventually you can set up your own promotion company. Where I've talked about working for somebody else, it's only as a means for entering the business and learning the ABCs of concert promotion. The size of the operation doesn't matter. The most important thing is to get into the industry—to immerse yourself in it. And if you can't even get into the concert business in your town, or into the related areas I've described, your next step should be to involve yourself in some other area of the entertainment industry. Do something. See if you have what it takes.

Learn the real function of an agent by working for an agency. Learn the cast of characters. Involvement is essential. Whether it's in a small concert hall or a large concert arena—indoors or outdoors—doesn't matter. Throw yourself into it. Nothing can help so much as being in the middle of it.

Don't expect to displace the major fixtures of the promotion industry. Don't look down on secondary or tertiary markets: secondary cities may offer less press emphasis and less ego satisfaction in terms of national or industry press, but you may make as much money as you can in a major market. In many instances you will make more money than you can in a major market, because your expenses are less.

Timing has to be right, too. When you feel you've gotten as much out of the apprenticeship as you can, when you feel stymied by the bigger promoters in town, when you've cultivated a group of investors and you're ready to hit them for a big promotion, you've got to initiate the change. *You* have to do it, not your wife, your girlfriend, or any of your business associates. When you feel that you understand the business, that you have your production skills and finances down, that you can accommodate a move, and that you can survive the competition, that's the time to move on.

8
Putting Together Capital

THERE ARE always people who want to be in show business: people who are impressed with the glamour of the industry, of being backstage, of being able to say to their friends, "I was the financial investor who made that show possible."

More often than not, these people are associated with serving as angels for Broadway productions. But wealthy people can be approached to invest in rock concerts. This chapter will help you learn how to sell these people.

If you're going for money to people who run standard businesses (and any business is more standard than the rock and roll business), perhaps the most important thing to keep in mind is that you mustn't frighten your potential investor. You mustn't frighten him with certain generalizations often made about rock people: that they're unpredictable, psychedelic, into crazy music, and that they have teenage orgies every night. Dispel the prejudices against rock and roll, and against yourself. Explain to the potential investor that although rock may be an irregular business, that it may have some idiosyncrasies, you are submitting a proposal that is devoid of all idiosyncrasies.

The targets of your quest for capital are businessmen: men who have made a lot of money and are looking for revenue-creating businesses, not tax shelters. Investors should be sold on the basis of receiving a quick, high-yield return for each dollar they invest.

Basically, there are two reasons why successful businessmen invest in rock. First, they see your concert as a pure business deal. You'll need hard-core data to make a sale. Second, and this is something you should know before you approach the potential investor, they are interested in the glamour of the rock industry. They want to be touched by the excitement of being backstage. They want to hear what Mick Jagger is really like. They want to be stars to their teenage daughters. Study which of these twin motivations—business or glamour—is predominant in your quarry, and adjust your selling routine accordingly.

Begin collecting data on a particular group or act you wish to promote by consulting the trade magazines. *Amusement Business*, a *Billboard* publication, has the most extensive concert information of any trade paper. It lists coliseum and arena grosses, the best grosses, and the most attractive grosses of the year. *Variety*, *Billboard*, and *Record World* also publish information about concert grosses and attendance. See appendixes D and E for sample listings from *Amusement Business* and *Billboard*.

Another source of data for selling your proposal to a potential investor is the record company. Find out how many records the attraction has sold in your area, along with information from local radio stations and record stores on consumer response. Contact the publicity department of the record company for a press kit, which contains biographical information, clippings, and photographs of the attraction.

You should also have a facility brochure to show the potential investor. Generally speaking, any supportive information you can get on the attraction, the hall, and how well rock music is received in the community, is very useful.

Now that you've assembled your information, the leading question to ask is, "Who should I go to?" There are really no listings that you can rely on. It's all word of mouth. You learn that so-and-so had the money, but he didn't have the facility, or that so-and-so is a good person to go to—he couldn't get attractions, he couldn't get facilities, but he wants in.

I've been successful in approaching regular retail business people and investment bankers. I've spoken to attorneys whose job it is always to keep an eye open for intelligent, revenue-creating opportunities for their wealthy clients. I think it's a waste of time, however, to approach artists or record companies. I also think it's a waste of time to go to a bank to secure financing for an individual concert. In general, I approach people who are not in the music business, who are speculators with spendable cash, who are not averse to speculating. I meet them at parties, through mutual friends, or I visit them in their office. They're individuals, not corporations. You can't deal with a bureaucracy in the concert business. You need individuals who can read a prospectus, talk to you person to person, and give you a quick reply.

In the standard deal between the investor and the promoter, the investor puts up all the money required to produce the show. Usually the investor gets his investment back from ticket sales first. Then the promoter and the investor each receive 50 percent of the profits. The promoter has to take the intitiative in making deals, not the investor. You get what you can: unlike banks, the concert business has no regulating bodies or established interest rates.

A key negotiating point is whether the promoter is entitled to a nonreturnable administrative fee covering the time and expertise he's put into the show. This administrative fee should be added to the promoter's PCA form and submitted to the potential investor along with other needed supporting documentation. It is a perfectly legitimate thing to ask for, and I strongly advocate that potential concert promoters put in for it. For a concert with a GP after taxes of $20,000, I'd budget an administrative fee of $1,000 to $1,500. If the GP after taxes if $50,000, I'd ask for $2,500 as an administrative fee.

Sometimes the investor or group of investors will ask the promoter to put up at least a token amount of money as proof that the promoter believes very strongly in the project. The promoter, in turn, is going to fight to have his administrative fee considered an off-the-top expense, rather than an advance against his 50 percent share of the profits. The investor will frequently push for 60 percent instead of 50 percent of the profits. My deals were usually close to fifty-fifty. However, if I had superstars that I knew were going to sell out, I took larger fees, gave up considerably less than 50 percent and in some cases didn't reimburse my investors 100 percent before we started participating.

The sample investor agreement found in appendix F was for a concert I promoted featuring Jethro Tull and Robin Trower at Shea Stadium in 1976. The investor agreed to loan my company $40,000, payable in three installments prior to the concert, in return for a 25 percent participation in the concert's net profits. Total expenses for the show, which included my company's repayment of the $40,000 loan plus an administrative fee for me, were not to exceed $268,500, plus possible overage payments to Jethro Tull and Robin Trower in the event of a near or complete sellout. Before we split the profits, the investor recaptured his $40,000 loan. If either Jethro Tull or Robin Trower failed to perform at Shea Stadium, I was obligated to reimburse the investor for talent costs. The essence of this contract, including other substantive points, was contained in a short letter agreement prepared by my lawyer and modified slightly by the investor. Despite the fact that it rained horribly at Shea Stadium on the day of the concert, this turned out to be an excellent deal for the investor, the attractions, and Howard Stein Enterprises.

When I failed in raising money, it was because I took things for granted. I assumed that a conservative business-man knew that Jefferson Starship were just unbelievably hot in Chicago, or that the Grateful Dead sold out every time they played New York. Assumptions can be disastrous. Show people how strong an act is with data. Prove it to them.

Some people are very effective wearing sneakers, torn blue jeans, and ponytails. Somebody may be investing in you because he thinks that, as a ponytailed, sneakered rock and roll person, you are an expert in that area. Being your-self is probably the best recommendation to make concern-ing what way to dress.

As far as what to sell, I've always primarily sold the at-traction when trying to put capital together for rock con-certs. You may think that your concept is unique, or that the facility is especially prime, but the attraction is the star. If you have an attraction that the investor has heard of, and in a positive way, your job will be much easier. You're going to require less backup information to prove the viability of that attraction. The more obscure the attraction, the more diffi-cult it will be to sell the act to wealthy individuals.

Protect yourself in dealing with potential investors. Your first consideration should be submitting a budget that you can meet. Try not to get penalized if you come in higher than you estimated. While you're doing the budget, I re-commend strongly that you give yourself an intelligent cushion—for me, it was simply adding 15 percent to every item in the budget—so that you look better with your in-vestors than you anticipated if you bring the concert in below cost.

Deep down, most investors figure that they're going to get killed when they speculate with money. If your initial experience with a group of investors is positive, chances are you've got yourself a permanent group. On the other hand, if you lose initially, chances are you've lost yourself a group. The first experience with a new group is absolutely vital.

Never deal as an individual with potential investors. Always be a corporation—a vital move for avoiding personal liability. If the company is going to go bankrupt, there is no reason why you as an individual should have to go bankrupt. Also, make sure that both the company and you, personally, are insured properly.

Don't lie to potential investors. Don't say that the show can't lose, or that emergencies don't happen. I wouldn't emphasize them, but I would admit to some of the problems that might occur before you're asked. Don't pretend to be a know-it-all, either. If you say to the potential investor, "These are the only possible problems that can happen," and the problem that does come up wasn't included on your list, you're in very serious hot water.

Admit to some of the aspects of the industry that make it somewhat dangerous, and agree that it's speculative. I would, however, stress one of the good points: the money comes in fast. If the date is two and a half months away, on the day of the concert you will know exactly where you stand. If the show succeeds, the profit will be in your pocket that evening, along with the recoupment of the investor's front money. It's clean, it's over on a specific date, and that's the end of it.

Individual concerts are too speculative for banks to get involved. However, if your plans call for owning a club, or buying or leasing a theater that can project tangible income based on ticket sales, concessions, whiskey, or facility rentals, at that point you can go to a bank or to financing companies.

In developing a business plan and projected profit and loss statement for an owned facility, I recommend that you project no more than 75 percent capacity of paying customers on an annual basis. Your profit, or income, will be arrived at by adding together ticket sales (average ticket price, times 75 percent capacity, times the number of days the facility will be open during the year), concession income (from cigarette machines, jukeboxes, and so on), estimated whiskey and food consumption, facility rentals (to other promoters, if that's your plan), and other income (e.g., a record company may want to record at your facility). Against these income projections you will have to itemize your total expenses: overhead, professional services, talent, equipment purchases, maintenance of the facility and equipment, labor, payroll taxes, and, in all likelihood, the mortgage on the facility. Project this statement of profit and loss (P&L) over a five-year period: if the bottom line profit looks healthy you may be able to secure a loan.

Don't be put off when you hear that people won't talk to you because they're not interested in entertainment deals. You've just got to find people who are at least receptive to sitting down and talking about music deals. You should also express to them that rock and roll is a better business, and a safer business, than the Broadway theater. Besides, if you need money to implement your promotion plans, and like most start-up promoters you don't have any, you don't have much choice other than to try.

9
Contracts and Riders

IN THEORY, it's essential to have a written understanding, or contract, for whatever business relationship exists among the concert promoter, the artist, and the agent. In practice, very often the contract is not signed by an attraction until after the engagement, or until it's too late to make any changes.

Many attractions, I think, purposely don't sign contracts. They want to keep their options open for a better deal from a bigger concert promoter, motion picture director, or prime-time TV special producer. However, verbal concert promotion agreements between the attraction and the promoter are usually held to be binding, since the standard operating condition of this industry involves telephone calls rather than written correspondence. If problems do come up, they often turn on a delicate point of law—namely, that a promoter gets his confirmations from the agency, which is really not a direct party in the contract. The typical artist copout in these cases is that "True, the agency said yes, but we, the attraction, whose signature (or voice) is needed to make the contract binding, didn't say yes."

The only recourse for being treated properly in the concert promotion business is to develop a reputation for being a major concert promoter. Major promoters don't get canceled out of concerts without replay dates. They don't get abused to the extent that novices, or disrespected promoters, do. The bigger you get, and the tighter your control over leading venues, the more respect you'll receive from agencies and attractions.

As a service to their union members, the American Federation of Musicians (AFM) and the American Guild of Variety Artists (AGVA) have put together standard artist engagement contracts (see appendixes G and H). Their basic purpose is to set the time, place, starting time, price, and payment conditions for a concert. Members of the AFM (instrumentalists) are expected to use the AFM contract; members of AGVA (vocalists) are expected to use the AGVA contract. If an attraction is not affiliated with either the AFM or AGVA, it will use an artist engagement contract prepared by the agency. In my ten-year promotion career, which spans more than 2,500 concerts, I have not had occasion to become an expert on these standard face contracts. Their purpose, in terms of industry practice, is to fix the principal players for the show, the stage and time of the event, and possibly ticket prices. They are not the center of controversy among promoters, attractions, and their lawyers, despite their length and legal obtuseness.

The real time and study that I've put into contracts has been focused on the contract rider, which is attached to the AFM/AGVA or agency contract. The rider describes the physical concert production in great detail. Every technical specification of the attraction—every service specification that the promoter must provide—should be spelled out in the concert rider blueprint, and gone over with the attraction's agent prior to the concert. If the promoter and agent are in accord over the terms of the rider, the relationship among the promoter, agency, and attraction should be trouble-free.

Some riders, for new artists, may be only two pages long. Others, for superstars, may contain thirty pages of orders (no other word will suffice) whose sybaritic completeness will astound the novice promoter. A two-page, basic rider for an opening or marginal act tells the promoter that the attraction requires a sound system, and usually gives the specifications in terms of power requirements and the number of microphones that sound system should have. It then becomes the responsibility of the promoter to lease that equipment from a local sound and light supply house, or to see to it that the facility can accommodate the act's own portable sound equipment, which the promoter must rent ⌐ngagement.

⌐ a new act, the rider usually calls for the promoter to two or three spotlights for the attraction, in addition lighting. Occasionally, start-up acts travel with su- and arrange to use the superstar's lights, sound, and ything the rider can do to clear up these organiza- teries is considered helpful to the promoter and on coordinator.

otally controlled, as is the whole industry, by The headliner will demand 100 percent sole ning that on a scale from 1 to 100 percent, can be larger than that of the headliner. ay ask for 50 percent special or 75 percent ng (i.e., 50 or 75 percent of the size of the me), but the final decision on how large the appears in newspaper ads and on the facility's reserved for the headliner.

eral, the promoter still has a certain amount of ith new acts, opening acts, or marginal acts who there alone. He can delete certain service requests he rider, such as limousines or a Madison Ave- pe buffet, without fear of reprisal. This power, how- ever, will be totally negated if the agent decides to impose his strength and take the act under his wing, or the headliner traveling with that act decides to support it. As soon as an industry "heavy" gets involved, the promoter's negotiating position becomes highly disproportionate.

The elements of a superstar concert rider can be truly mindboggling, although several major acts base their rider terminology on a desire to separate the business of performing an engagement from the before and after pleasures of wine, parties, and other personal delectations. Rather than paraphrase the artist concert rider that is contained in appendix I, I feel it is appropriate to comment generally on the gross amount of monetary waste that accompanies the more outlandish rider requests.

The concert riders of today seem to express an almost perverse desire to be fed, driven, and pandered to in a way that is absolutely unnecessary. The amount of food that is requested for the few hours that the attraction is backstage cannot be eaten. The amount of liquor that is required cannot be drunk. The number of limousines that are ordered cannot be utilized in such a short time period. These extraordinary items not only lessen the amount of money a promoter can make; they can also cut quite heavily into the attraction's profit potential, especially from overages.

I question whether it is necessary (some acts apparently think it is) to furnish gourmet meals from morning until night for their road crew. I wonder whether, years from now, the attraction who insisted on a $2,000 after-concert snack might rather have settled for a $200 snack, and pocketed the difference. I remember one attraction that required a case of Dom Perignon backstage after each·engagement. The attraction couldn't even spell Dom Perignon, but they knew they wanted it. Most of that attraction's engagements ended up with members of the road crew taking bottles of Dom Perignon, shaking them up, and having mock seltzer-bottle fights. This is not a unique case in the annals of after-concert ways of blowing additional profits.

In certain cases it's not even that the act wants the limousines, or desires to eat cavier or drink champagne. It's a macabre illustration of how some artists feel they must keep step with the Joneses (e.g., "Well, if that act used to be the biggest act in the world before I came on the scene and replaced them, how do I prove to myself and to the world and to the agency that I'm bigger?"). The essence of what I'm advocating to the artist is that less is better. Forget the champagne that will never be drunk. Forget the fourth and fifth limousines. Be satisfied with a deluxe hotel suite, rather than an entire hotel floor. Fame being as fleeting as it is in the rock business, artists should save money for the not-too-distant future when they actually might need some personal assets. These are some of the things that artists should think about when their attorney is drafting next year's concert rider.

What I do think is an essential element in a major attraction's rider is clear, concise information dealing with how large the stage should be, how many semivans need to be unloaded, where the audio mixing platform, speakers, and stagelights should be located, how many security personnel the attraction will need backstage, what type of dressing room accommodations the act would like, and any other data that will enable the promoter to quantify his basic technical and living necessities for that show. This knowledge, in turn, will help the production coordinator decide how many stagehands to use for the unloading and set-up of equipment, how many fork lifts to use, and whether added backstage security should be hired. A well-conceived concert rider will prevent logistical and technical problems from happening on the day of the show, simply by calling attention several weeks earlier to manpower needs and basic comfort needs.

When a promoter receives a rider, he should go over every line very carefully. The best way to modify a rider is for the promoter to call the agency well in advance of the concert, and explain why he has a problem with a certain paragraph, line, or word. If the agent agrees to the change, the promoter should immediately delete or change the condition in the rider, initial the change, and return the rider to the agent for his initial. As a rule, if there is anything you want to modify in the rider, don't change it and then send it back changed or altered without speaking to the agent or the attraction first.

Superstars have contracts that virtually protect them from everything, and protect the promoter from nothing. In theory, the attraction and the promoter should submit riders to each other, but even before the superstar reigned supreme, my production riders were almost never signed. Sometimes they were just detached from the contract package and thrown away.

In the event of an act of God, or force majeure, that prevents a concert from occurring because of forces that are greater than anything an agent, personal manager, promoter, or attraction can handle, the act is always protected. Legally, the attraction doesn't have to perform. Usually, if it's a conscionable attraction, and there's a blackout or a storm that prohibits anyone from getting to the facility, or the facility burns down, the attraction will credit the promoter the monies it's received (it's almost impossible to get a refund from an agency) and make up the concert. Replay commitments, if they're not already expressed in the rider, should be called to the attention of the agent by the promoter and reduced to writing. The least you should have in your relationship with the artists and the agency is a chance to wipe out the promotion and advertising costs incurred by the canceled date.

Some promoters add various forms of hedonistic delights to their service function with an act, but that was never my style. I've never been required to be a pimp or dope connection for an attraction. Besides, if an act that makes $50,000 a night and is lauded by all the young women in the world has trouble getting a date, I'm hardly the person who can solve that problem.

The way you deal with the concert rider is going to determine how the agency and management talk about you as a professional when they walk away from the engagement. It's going to determine whether that act and agent want to deal with you again. In fact, it's going to be the beginning of your reputation as a professional.

The biggest thing to avoid is surprising the act. The real disaster happens when the promoter assumes that, instead of a B-3 organ, which he couldn't get, a C-3 organ will do, or that a Lincoln Continental can replace a six-door Mercedes Benz. Even if you've given the act something that is better than they requested, usually the act prefers the consistency of what they've seen on the ten dates before. Don't surprise the act. Speak constantly to the road manager; speak to the personal manager; speak to the agency on a regular basis.

Deal with the rider line by line. Take care of any changes long in advance of the concert. Let the hall and the unions know that if you submit certain specifications, you want those specifications dealt with to the letter. If you want to impress an attraction with how good a promoter you are, if they want three bottles of Courvoisier VSOP, give them three bottles. If they want a stage that's four and one-half feet high, make sure it's four and one-half feet high, not five feet or four feet.

The agency will want things from the promoter in a hurry. They'll want your deposit, your signature on hand, and a confirmation letter. After that, things slow down. The agency may never sign the contract. While you're waiting, make sure that you have a copy of the attraction's concert rider. It is your blueprint for success.

Too much is made about the importance of contracts and lawyers in this business. The important thing is to perform under duress, to show the attraction, manager, and agency that you're a major promoter, a major talent, and a good person to work with. If you do what the concert rider tells you to do, if you pay the act when you're supposed to and don't cheat them, and if the audience doesn't try to hurt the attraction (they shouldn't be able to, if your security is adequate), you'll discover that the place for most contracts—not including the rider—is the promoter's filing cabinet.

10
Tips on Selling Tickets

PUTTING TICKETS on sale may strike the novice concert promoter as being one of the more perfunctory aspects of the business. In reality, selling tickets is an important indicator to the public and to the attraction of the promoter's degree of professionalism. Here are some of the things I've learned about selling tickets that may be of help in your career.

As with so much of this artist-oriented industry, the approach to selling tickets depends on the drawing power of the attraction. If the artist is unknown, the promoter should make tickets available in as many places as possible. Put the tickets on sale at least five weeks prior to the concert. Offer the least amount of resistance to the potential audience by making tickets available at Ticketron outlets, agencies, the promoter's box office, the facility's box office, and by mail order. Make it as easy as possible to buy tickets.

If you can get away with it without alienating a super attraction, try tagging their newspaper ads with miniannouncements that "Appearing soon is [Unknown Artist Sensation]," or something to that effect. Try getting approval for a trailer at the end of a radio commercial that says, "Next attraction at [the facility] is [New Unknown Attraction]." Seek out as much free advertising, as much cooperative advertising, and as many tie-ins, album giveaways, posters, and flyers as possible. Really try to do an intensive promotional campaign. You're going to need it.

Tickets for medium-sized acts and superstars should also be placed on sale five weeks prior to the event. One of the reasons to get started early with ticket sales for these established groups is to gauge whether there is sufficient demand to do a second, or stretch, concert with the attraction. Very often, if the tickets sell out quickly and the promoter makes the act aware of the swift sellout, the act can be coerced into doing another show. Putting tickets up for sale five weeks in advance allows the promoter ample time to test the demand of the audience, negotiate the stretch performance, and organize the entire new show. There are, however, some basic risks in attempting to double your luck in the concert promotion business.

If you sell out one concert and book the act for a second concert that does only 60 or 65 percent of capacity, even though they've played to that many more people the act will walk away thinking, "The promoter made us do a second show, and it didn't go clean. It didn't sell out. It was humiliating to play to so many empty seats." An act will be more pleased with the promoter if he sells out one show completely, and turns thousands of people away. The best approach, which is also the most conservative, is not to do a second show unless every last ticket for the first show has sold out really early, and at an unusually fast pace. In this business you're only as good as the last show you promoted: do your best to make sure that last concert was jammed to capacity, rather than half-filled with unhappy customers and an unhappy act.

Medium-sized attractions and major headliners should also go through the entire ticket distribution system. Again, you want to make it easy for people to obtain tickets for these middle-level groups, whose guarantees may already be so high that it's absolutely essential for the show to sell out. But real superstars, acts that are so strong that they can get everybody from the surrounding area to converge on one place to buy tickets, do not need, and may not want to use, the ticket distribution system. All that may be required for these attractions is the facility's box office, adequate security precautions, and an understanding of how the act wants their tickets to be sold.

Style means a lot at this stratospheric level of the business. The promoter knows that the concert will be an automatic sellout, and so does the attraction. The question is, simply, how to sell tickets in a way that is unique? One way this striving to be unique has translated into reality is the offering of tickets through direct mail only. Another approach is to be totally democratic: place a full-page announcement in the newspaper, get on the radio, and put tickets up for sale in the usual outlets.

Of course, the most sensational approach is to sell tickets at one location, the facility's box office. If it's The Rolling Stones, you know you're going to get publicity. You know you're going to see people lifted up and passed down to the front of the ticket line over the heads of other people. You know you're going to create excitement for that event that will drive every kid for a hundred miles around insane. Selling tickets this way is one of the high points of any promoter's career. There are not, however, many groups with the drawing power to risk this media event approach.

When and if your chance to work with a Rolling Stones–type superstar attraction ever comes, make sure you take adequate crowd control precautions. Make contact with the local police department and the facility's own security. Put up your police barriers. Have some uniformed security present at all times. Check with the facility manager to see whether you're going to be charged for boarding up glass windows and doors. Ask whether you can be insured for injuries that occur during the wait in line. If you're trying to create hysteria, you'd better be able to prevent any hysterical acts of aggression directed toward either the facility or your potential customers.

Scalpers, the people who buy up blocks of seats and sell them at inflated prices to people in desperate need of attending the show, are not really a prime concern of the concert promoter. I certainly would not like to see young people having to spend $100 or more to see their favorite rock and roll star. Very often, in fact, I have done shows for which announcements are made that tickets are available, but no more than four tickets per person will be sold. These anti-scalper tactics can be quite effective. But as a promoter, you're always afraid. You don't want to do anything that slows down your sales or jeopardizes a sellout. In secondary or tertiary markets, I am frankly not that concerned about whether or not scalping goes on. As a promoter, I'm more concerned with selling out the concert.

Some events may lend themselves to selling tickets at discount prices, or offering reduced rates for block sales, but I've never discounted a rock concert. Kids will either be willing to pay the fair market price for a ticket to see a major attraction, with an opening act or marginal act thrown in as support, or the promoter won't be able to give tickets away. If time is to be spent in determining ticket prices for rock concerts, it should be spent analyzing what your competitors are charging in similar venues, and deciding whether to charge that price or slightly less.

As for refunds, my policy was to return money if people wanted to redeem their tickets for canceled performances. But to avoid the nuisance of processing an occasional refund request, I routinely rubber-stamped my tickets with the legend, "This ticket is not refundable."

The manner in which tickets go on sale may very well be controlled by the headliner's agency. In any case, whether the promoter is following orders or designing his own ticket-selling campaign, it is important to communicate openly and frequently on ticket sales with the agency. If tickets aren't moving, the agency should be informed immediately. There may be time, if the tickets are put on sale early enough, to make any necessary corrections in procedures.

One final comment: if it appears likely that the show is going to be a total fiasco, the promoter must be prepared to absorb that loss without losing his cool. No concert promoter is smart enough to select 100 percent winners. Neither, for that matter, are the major booking agencies and personal managers. What separates the financially successful promoters from the marginally successful promoters, aside from their access to prime talent, is their ability to take an occasional loss, spring back, and be ready to service another attraction from the same agency. If you can't stand taking a beating, the concert promotion business is not for you.

11
Advertising and Publicity

VARIOUS COMPONENTS go into the design and execution of a concert advertising campaign. First there is pure advertising. This consists of newspaper ads, posters, stickers, radio commercials, perhaps television commercials, and special advertising gimmicks, such as skywriting. Second, there is publicity. The job of the publicist is to get newspaper, radio, and television coverage of upcoming events, such as a rock concert or the release of a new album. The selling tools in public relations are the press kit, which contains biographical information about the artist, photographs, and recent newspaper clippings, and the telephone, used to make contact with newspaper editors, television producers, and radio personalities.

Concert promoters must pay either all or part of the cost of buying advertising space or time for a concert. They also may be asked to pay part of the cost of the independent publicity firm or person who normally handles the artist's concert activities—if not, they may want to hire a public rela-

tions staff person for their office, or retain a local PR professional for special events. This chapter will suggest ways to
hold advertising costs to a minimum, and to "think smart"
about the role of advertising and publicity in the concert
business.

Most superstars, in order to present a controlled, superprofessional image, have top public relations firms design
their newspaper ads and write copy for their media commercials. These ads will be given to the promoter several
days prior to the start of the ad campaign, along with directions on where they should be placed and how often they
should appear. Normally, the superstar (or else the record
company) pays for the production of camera-ready artwork
to go to the printer, and finished commercials ready to be
played on the radio in a nationally orchestrated advertising
campaign.

All other attractions—start-up, middle-level, and major
artist—will expect the promoter to design newspaper ads
for them. These are usually fairly simple designs featuring
the names of the headliner and support attraction in bold
headline type, the date, place, and time of the concert, the
location of the facility, a breakdown of ticket prices, and a
telephone number to call for information. For the top of the
ad the promoter should have an attractive logo designed
that reads, "[Concert Promoter] Presents." This logo should
be used as a theme for every concert you produce.

One of the best ways to save money in buying newspaper
space is by using strip ads. These long, single-column ads
make it possible to advertise more than a half-dozen upcoming concerts at one time. The strip ad might cost a total of
$1,500, but it is far less expensive than taking out separate
two- or three-column ads (still pretty inconspicuous) for
each act. Strip ads have the depth to command the reader's
attention, and will become a looked-at feature in the
paper's music section if they're run on a regular basis. Of

course, the promoter has to have a volume of business before he can use the strip-ad approach to his advantage.

The person employed by a concert promoter to prepare newspaper ads is called a graphics designer. This person is usually a freelance commercial artist who will quote the promoter a flat fee for designing a newspaper ad, ordering the type, and pasting it together on a hard board called a mechanical. Some of the more talented graphics designers work for record companies, but they often are interested in moonlighting for special clients after normal working hours. A good finished mechanical may run anywhere from $150 to $300, including design, type, and pasteup.

Newspaper advertising rates will vary depending on when the ad is scheduled to run (Sundays or weekdays), the location of the ad in the newspaper, the size of the ad, and the frequency of runs. Rates can be obtained by contacting the display advertising department of the newspaper and describing the ad over the telephone. Most newspapers charge national or local advertising rates that are not negotiable. Full payment is normally required in advance, by certified check, until such time as the promoter establishes credit with the paper.

An effective money-saving technique is for the promoter to start his own in-house advertising agency. The cost is minimal—a couple of dollars to notarize a DBA (Doing Business As) form, available at any leading stationery store— but the savings can be quite dramatic: 15 percent off the regular price of newspaper ads and radio and TV commercials for in-house ad agency accounts. So long as the promoter is able to pay for advertising "up front," the legitimacy of his in-house agency standing will rarely be questioned. A sample DBA form, filled out for Howard Stein Media, is shown in appendix J.

Newspaper ads should be the earliest form of advertising for a concert. I like to run newspaper ads five weeks before the concert, at the same time tickets are placed on sale, giving my conservative audience plenty of time to plan for the event. Newspaper ads are usually one-time affairs, two times at most. Radio, on the other hand, is a frequency advertising medium. Most artists will want to advertise their concert twenty, thirty, forty, or more times on the radio, spreading their commercials over several leading stations in town. Radio should be used later than newspapers, perhaps only two or three weeks before the show.

Radio is one area where the promoter may be able to influence the direction and cost of the advertising campaign. Since radio can be incredibly expensive—as much as $300 a minute in major U.S. cities—it behooves the promoter to shop around for stations that deliver the most ad responses per dollar, and recommend to the attraction a preferred schedule of local radio time buys.

Rather than use the top-rated AM station, I prefer investigating specially formatted FM stations that play the artist's type of music exclusively, and appeal to audiences that fit the attraction's concert demographics (i.e., predominantly male or female, teenagers or young adults, white or black, high school or college educated). Rates for these smaller stations may run only $30 to $60 a minute, yet provide the same results—sometimes better—as the more heavily used AM stations, where commercials tend to get lost in the shuffle and the audience makeup is less specific.

When shopping around for a radio station, you should first find out if the station will honor your 15 percent agency discount. You will discover that some radio stations are willing to do more for your business than others. Some stations, for instance, will be willing to award you bonus spots, or free commercials, if you sign up for a minimum number of paid commercials (usually at least fifteen a week). Some stations will be willing to switch all of your commercials into prime-time listening areas, as opposed to the normal practice of spreading commercials over prime-time and off-peak hours. Some stations will be willing to do on-air promotions for your concert, such as offering free tickets to the first twenty people who call in, or free record albums, or T-shirts. Some radio stations can be influenced by the promoter in these ways; others cannot. The best way to find out, and save money while you're at it, is to shop around early, see which stations offer you the best deal, and spread your commercials over the least expensive but most targeted stations playing the artist's kind of music.

Commercial copy is usually prepared by the radio station for approval by the promoter, unless the attraction has already written and produced a commercial. Normally, there is no charge for commercials produced at the radio station. Copy can either be read live or produced with the artist's recent album music in the background.

After a contract has been signed between the promoter and the radio station, the promoter will be informed of the times when his commercials are scheduled to be broadcast. Listen for your commercials. Make sure they play on schedule, that their information is accurate, and that they're read properly by the disc jockey (i.e., no laughing and not too much ad-libbing). Reputable radio stations will issue make-good commercials for any goofs on their part.

Generally speaking, I don't think television advertising is a very effective medium for rock concerts. Most serious rock fans don't need TV announcements to make them aware of upcoming live performances: either they've heard about it on the radio, seen the newspaper ad, read something in *Rolling Stone* magazine, or found out through the most effective advertising medium of all—word of mouth.

In reality, most TV ads for rock shows are poorly disguised hype campaigns for the attraction. They may want the general television audience to see how big they've grown. They may want other entertainment moguls in the TV audience to see their power, their presence, and the excitement they can generate in fifteen or thirty seconds of videotape. It's fine if an attraction wants to advertise its availability to do bigger and better things, but I don't think rock promoters should be asked to shoulder this unnecessary financial burden. If it's an important attraction, the least you should do is try getting the artist's record company to pay part of the cost. For smaller groups, I wouldn't even think of TV campaigns; put your money where the underground audience first discovers potential rock superstars, in posters, flyers, and T-shirts.

Public relations, or publicity, can be a very treacherous area for start-up promoters. Getting publicity requires the ability to develop interesting story angles about the attraction, and the time to pitch these stories aggressively to newspaper and magazine editors, the producers of radio and television talk shows, and disc jockeys. Good PR can make a big difference in helping sell out a concert. Most super attractions, in fact, don't even need to advertise. The publicity they've received over the years is so intense, and so omnipresent, that even the most casual announcement of an upcoming event will do the trick.

Promoters shouldn't have to get personally involved with publicity, but very often, when a show appears to be dying, they have no choice. The cardinal rule, when it comes time to don one's publicity hat, is to first coordinate with the attraction's personal manager, record company, and public relations firm. Find out what they've done, whom they've talked to, and the reasons they haven't been able to get publicity. Then, if you have personal contacts with local critics or reporters, get on the phone and remind these media persons that [the act] is performing in the next few days, and they're invited to attend.

Do not, however, go beyond this professional courtesy. Don't damage your credibility by hyping the act excessively, or lying. State the facts, add that extra invitation (which is really why you're calling—reporters are inundated with requests), but maintain a professional distance. Here, as in so many areas of the music business, an act can and should survive only on its own merits, and the merits of its supporting management.

If you're dealing with a true superstar, the so-called automatic sellout, the tone of the advertising campaign will be to make a simple announcement. Even though the act could probably sell out through word-of-mouth advertising, the artist's concert rider may instruct the promoter to buy a quarter-page, half-page, or full-page ad in the Sunday entertainment section of the most important local newspaper, and to buy spots on two of the major rock radio stations for at least two weeks. Any suggestions of changes in the superstar's advertising campaign must be cleared with the act's agency and/or management.

Major artists either do very little or very much advertising: very little if they just want the promoter to sell out the date for them; very much if they want to make a point about how big they are. Some attractions, on achieving sellout, may ask the promoter to take out an additional full-page ad that reads, "We thank you, [City where concert is being held], for helping us sell out this show." The conditions for who should pay for this ad, and when it should be taken out, should be spelled out during the precontract signing stage. As with TV commercials, I don't think the promoter should be expected to pay 100 percent for this veiled image-building plug for the attraction.

Quite a bit of advertising in today's business is paid for on a cooperative basis. Co-op advertising means that, in the case of a newspaper ad, the artist's record company may pay all or part of the cost, provided the ad contains some mention of the artist's new album. Record companies may also be asked by the artist's personal manager to subsidize publicity expenses, radio commercials, and the printing of posters and stickers. Occasionally the manager invests his own money in additional advertising, if he can't get it from the record company and he feels it's really necessary.

Much of the burden has been reduced in terms of finances, but learning where to advertise in a local market, and developing publicity contacts, is still a tricky, time-consuming business. One thing is for certain: advertising and publicity can either make or break a concert. Learning the right way to do it, at an affordable price, will take years of trial-and-error experience.

12

The Hours Before the Concert

AS I HAVE ALREADY EXPRESSED many times, the concert promotion business today has been reduced to a service industry. The artist's concert rider will tell the promoter exactly what to do: how big the stage should be, where to position the mixing platform, what type of food to order for the act and the act's road crew, how much security an act needs backstage, how many limousines to use, and so forth. The purpose of this chapter is to translate this production blueprint into affirmative action by walking the reader through an actual preconcert operation. I'll also offer some practical tips on how eleventh-hour crises, the scourge of all novice promoters, can be avoided.

Planning the hours prior to the concert actually begins several weeks earlier, when the promoter puts in a call to his boss for the night of the show: the attraction's road manager. He can be reached through the personal manager's office, and usually will have to return your call, since he literally is always on the road. The purpose of this introductory conversation is to make the road manager aware that you, the concert promoter, will be working with him soon. You might want to say something like, "Hi, this is Howard Stein. An engagement with [the attraction] has been confirmed for the Seattle arena on October 3. I'm looking forward to working with you. Now, are there any special things I should keep in mind before I get the concert rider? Any problems I can avoid by having an early conversation with you?"

The road manager will appreciate this courtesy call, and talk to the promoter not only about technical considerations, but also the attraction's general mood: whether they're up or down, sane or insane, and other personal information that may be of considerable importance in terms of making the attraction feel comfortable with the promoter and the engagement.

Once the promoter does receive the concert rider, copies of it should be made immediately and sent to the facility manager, head of the stagehands, and the promoter's own production coordinator. The promoter should call these people in a couple of days, make sure they've received their riders, and go over any special trouble areas with them. Promoters should never assume that anybody actually reads concert riders. It is their responsibility to study the rider in minute detail and bring potential problems to the attention of others.

A key to having a concert go off clean, or trouble-free, is to prepare a list of telephone numbers where important production personnel can be contacted on the day of the concert. The road manager, facility manager, production manager for the act (if a separate individual from the road manager), production coordinator for the hall, head electrician, head of the union stagehands and in-house security, and the person in charge of external security, should all be included on this list. Find out where these people can be reached at any given moment during the entire day—not just their office numbers, but the number of their hotel lobby, or restaurant, or place of outside meeting. If trouble does come up, you must be able to get through to the persons on this list with a minimum of delay. Don't keep these numbers on individual pieces of scrap paper—prepare a master, preferably typewritten, list.

Another important element in preproduction planning, especially if you're working in a new facility, is to try to gauge the competence of the people in that building. Based on your feeling for a particular group of individuals, you may want to make contact with potential backup persons. This applies not only to the stagehands, electricians, and in-house security, but also to outside services such as portable stage companies, caterers, and limousine rental agencies. Calling in last-minute substitute services has saved any number of professional concert promoters—including myself—from total financial disaster. If you feel you have to take backup precautions, contact these people prior to the day of the concert. Add their names to the list of telephone contacts.

The day of the concert can begin as early as 12:00 A.M., if the facility is available for early set-up. (Bear in mind, however, that if you want the facility's stagehands to construct the stage immediately after a basketball or hockey game, this is considered an extraordinary time to work, and the promoter will be hit with time-and-a-half or double-time charges by the stagehands union.) Most halls are geared for early morning load-ins beginning at 8:00 A.M. A superprofessional production team, such as accompanies the Rolling Stones, Yes, or Peter Frampton, can unload three semivans, construct a stage, transport equipment onto the stage, position that equipment on the stage, install overhead sound, lights, and backdrops, clean up the facility, and position the mixing platform for a sound check during a six-hour period, from 8:00 A.M. to 4:00 P.M. Normally it takes two hours to unload the equipment, two hours to position it onstage, and five to six hours to rig the backdrops, sound, and lights from the ceiling of the facility. The work force needed to assemble a large arena show numbers between fourteen and twenty able-bodied men.

Who these men should be, the unions they are affiliated with, and the policy of each facility with respect to setting up live concerts must be researched in advance by the concert promoter or the promoter's production coordinator. Knowing which union is in charge of a particular element of the production at a particular time, and who to talk to if there's a problem in that area, is absolutely essential if a large-scale production is to be completed on schedule.

During the load-in and set-up of equipment, the general of the troops is the road manager. The lieutenant general is the concert promoter. The colonels are the attraction's production manager, the promoter's production coordinator, and the facility's production manager (the facility manager is an official observer of the proceedings). The captain is the promoter's stage manager, whose jurisdiction covers the area from the stage to the trucks. The sergeants are the foremen of the stagehands, Teamsters, and road crew—who are the privates. In this man's army, the privates should each be of equal importance: they will certainly have to work together, and they must be able to get along. The stagehands, Teamsters, and road crew will be deployed by the road manager in consultation with the heads of the various in-house unions. Actual determination of how much work the roadie can do, and how much work the union stagehand will permit that roadie to do, depends on the attitude of the different privates to each other (i.e., arrogance will be met with arrogance), and the realities of putting the show together (i.e., the stagehands don't know the proper order for screwing in the stagelights—they will have to take direction from the road crew).

Parking permits should be secured for the semivans, if they haven't been already, as they drive up to the facility load-in area. At 8:00 A.M. the production crew will gather for the first time as a unified team. The production crew may consist of union stagehands, nonunion helpers (if permitted), Teamsters, and the attraction's road crew. After a quick review of house policies, the road manager will tell the men the order in which the trucks are to be unloaded. Ideally, the sound and light equipment is unloaded first. If the facility has a contract with the Teamsters union, the job of unloading this equipment and transporting it to the stage is reserved exclusively to the Teamsters. Otherwise, the equipment is unloaded and transported to the stage by the stagehands.

Most facilities have service ramps that lead to the back of the stage. These ramps make it very easy to unload equipment from the trucks and move it near the stage. There are, unfortunately, a number of major arenas, including Madison Square Garden, whose ramps are too narrow to accommodate semivans. Several more Teamsters and at least two fork lifts will be needed at these halls to compensate for the additional time it takes to unload the trucks and get equipment to the stage. Load-in factors such as this should be researched and brought to the attention of the attraction's agency prior to signing a contract. The difference between one fork lift, one fork life operator, and fourteen stagehands, and two fork lifts, two fork lift operators, and eighteen stagehands, can well exceed $1,000. If these legitimate production expenses aren't computed in the Total Production Cost, along with other expenses on the PCA form, they will probably be deducted 100 percent from the promoter's potential profit.

The stage is constructed by the stagehands. If the act is traveling with its own portable stage, the road crew may help the stagehands unpack and install it. The next major item to be installed is the act's lighting truss. The truss is a large, rectangular maze of pipes to which the stagelights are connected. I've worked with trusses that are forty feet across by thirty feet deep, and weigh several tons. Most major acts today fly their lights from the ceiling of the facility. Several roadies, as well as the facility's in-house riggers, will take charge of attaching the stagelights to the truss and hoisting the truss into position. Once the lighting truss has been secured, the sound system goes up, thus minimizing sightline problems for the audience and allowing the promoter and the attraction to maximize the seating capacity of the hall.

Finally, the backdrops are sent up on cables and properly positioned at the rear of the stage. In my experience, it can take as many as five or six hours to position all the lines that hold the sound, lights, and backdrops for an arena show.

Electrical equipment must be Underwriter Laboratory (UL) approved. As a condition of the facility rental agreement, the facility's chief electrician will have the right to inspect each electronic device scheduled to be used for the show. The chief electrician should be available for consultation from the 8:00 A.M. load-in through the conclusion of the concert. Either the road manager or the attraction's production manager should have in his possession copies of UL certificates of approval for the electronic equipment.

As stated earlier, it is imperative that the Teamsters, stagehands, and road crew get along with each other. The main reason work stoppages sometimes occur is because one or more members of the attraction's road crew develop an attitude of superiority toward the stagehands. Stagehands should never be ordered to do anything: the correct way to talk to a stagehand is to make a suggestion or ask a favor. Stagehands should never be told to work faster: there is method to the madness, from the stagehands' point of view, of using paint brushes instead of paint rollers, or using individual thumbtacks instead of a staple gun.

If the road crew want to get their job over with and relax for a few hours before the concert, they must also recognize that the stagehands, in their own way, must protect their jobs. Proper scheduling of the attraction's road crew is one way to prevent altercations during the preconcert hours. Members of the road crew, who may work as many as fifty days in a row without stopping, should have their jobs rotated. Their physical and mental health is usually looked after by an attentive road manager. If they're acting irritable, perhaps it would be better to give them the day off and hire additional stagehands, or at least try to discover and remedy the cause of irritability. Hiring an additional stagehand to relieve pressure on a road crew member is one of the more familiar requests made by road managers that alter the basic concert rider agreement. It's one of the reasons why I recommended adding 15 percent to the outside costs of stagehands on the PCA form.

When pressure buildups occur, as they almost invariably do, the road manager and the promoter's production coordinator should be on the scene immediately, acting as lay psychologists and philosophers. Violence cannot be condoned, but neither can work stoppages that can delay a concert for two, three, or four hours. They should be avoided at all costs.

In my experience, as much as 10 percent of what the attraction calls for in its concert rider will be modified on the day of the show. The most common last-minute requests are for additional riggers, stagehands, and fork lifts. Occasionally, a defective speaker or amplifier may need to be replaced. There may also be slight changes in the food and beverage department, or a sudden shift in preference from Cadillac to Mercedes-Benz limousines.

Whatever the change, the road manager's approach to the promoter is generally very sane. He understands that the potential problem has not arisen because of any fault on the part of the promoter, but due either to a miscalculation on the part of whoever was responsible for putting together the attraction's concert rider, or to a sudden whim of the attraction. My production coordinator usually decided on the spot what type of deal to work out with the road manager vis-à-vis these additional production items. If the act was very important and the concert was certain to make a lot of money for all of us, I might be willing to absorb 100 percent of the additional costs. If advance ticket sales were less healthy and the group only marginal, I might be willing to go fifty-fifty or less with the attraction, depending on the amount of the adjusted bill. For new attractions, I was much less willing to bend, although even here the promoter sometimes has no choice but to accede to the act's request, if the concert would otherwise be in jeopardy. Expect last-minute changes. If you've done your homework, you should have backup telephone numbers and access to vital services without having to burst a blood vessel. It's a part of the business you must learn to take in stride.

During the preconcert hours, the concert promoter and his production coordinator should be absolutely mobile. Quite a few road managers have begun to use skateboards to get around the inside of major facilities in order to save time and energy. I personally think this is a good idea. Time is of the essence when problems come up; the quicker you can get to the heart of the problem and solve it, the better.

Generous portions of Danish and coffee should be served to the production crew at 8:00 A.M. During their lunch hour, members of the union stagehands will either eat out or bring box lunches. The road crew, on the other hand, must be catered to by the concert promoter. Rider requests for the road crew's meals run the gamut from cold sandwiches and an assortment of sodas to full-course hot meals.

I liked to disguise my catered meals as best I could. Some of the union stagehands may resent the fact that they aren't eating as well as the road crew. The promoter's response to the stagehands with respect to this complaint is that the promoter is paying the stagehands' salaries, and it is not a condition of their union contract that the promoter provide each stagehand with a catered meal. Still, it's better to be discreet about ordering in sirloin steaks for lunch. Food is something that should not be flaunted in the face of stage-hands who may be working just as hard as the road crew, but are eating considerably less.

Also on the matter of food, I strongly recommend that novice promoters lock the door to the room where the at-traction's catered spread is delivered. Sometimes I would even post a guard at this door to prevent the stagehands from getting inside. A twenty-five-pound assortment of ex-pensive cold cuts can be consumed by a hungry stage crew in a matter of minutes. If possible, hold off on delivering the food until you know that the artist is on his way to the facili-ty for a sound check. Then smuggle it in as secretly as you can.

When the artists drive up to the facility in their limou-sines, the concert promoter should be one of the first people to welcome them. But after a quick "Howdie, how are you, is there anything I can get for you prior to the concert?" the artist should be left alone. I don't think it's a good policy for promoters to get too friendly with artists, unless the act wishes to strike up the friendship. If there's nothing to say except small talk, the promoter should get back to his main business, and leave the artists to theirs.

By this time (approximately 4:00 P.M.), the facility should be ready. Stage props in need of repair will have been fixed by the road crew and placed in position. The art-ist's personal equipment and costumes will have been un-loaded and placed in the artist's dressing room, with at least one security person guarding the entrance to this area. The road crew will have installed the mixing platform some-where in the middle of the orchestra section, about one hun-dred feet from the stage. When the artists are ready, they will walk onstage for a brief sound check. If everything is "go," the artists will leave the facility and return to their hotel rooms. At about 6:45 P.M. the doors of the facility will be opened for an 8:00 P.M. show.

More often than not, things won't be "go" exactly at 4:00 P.M. Some diplomacy will be needed to keep the artist in check, either backstage or in the wings, while the remaining heavy construction in the auditorium takes place. Small details, such as positioning curtains around the stage or setting up minor stage props, should wait until after the sound check. But the stage lights and sound must be completely installed prior to the artist's tuning onstage

Even though there should be absolute silence during the sound check, it's often impossible to stop the stagehands from making some noise. If the artist is especially finicky, the promoter should tell the stagehands to stop work during the sound check, and pay them additional money for their extra time on the job. Of course, if the promoter feels the act is not that strong, he may be able to persuade the act that construction work must continue during the sound check, thus avoiding extra payments to the stagehands.

The only person who really knows how long it's going to take to finish setting up and complete the sound check is the road manager. The hall manager will ask the concert promoter when to open the doors. The concert promoter, in turn, must seek guidance from the road manager. It is very common to delay opening the doors by a half-hour.

The attraction determines how it's going to arrive at the facility for show time. Major groups will probably want to be seen in limousines. Superstars, like the Rolling Stones, The Who, or Peter Frampton, may want to disguise their entry by using a hotdog or catering truck, or an old jalopy. It's impossible to conceal the superstar completely from his public, but kids do think twice about mobbing a nondescript hotdog truck. Usually, because their arrival occurs outside, I assign city police to escort the stars inside the facility. Once inside, the artists are surrounded by internal plainclothes and T-shirted security.

Beyond the road manager, who often assigns classroom-type grades to the promoter on his performance that day, the artist is the ultimate individual to satisfy. This is some-times almost impossible to do. I remember, for example, a concert I produced with a major artist in Minneapolis that nearly died fifteen minutes into the show. The artist, who had insisted that there be absolutely no lights in the ceiling during his performance, was incensed that a tiny blue fire emergency light was still on. This was not the time to stroke the artist's ego. My production coordinator, who was fa-miliar with the facility, told the artist that there was a fire ordinance in Minneapolis requiring that the blue light stay on. We showed the artist a letter signed by the governor of Minnesota saying that the light must remain on. Finally, my production coordinator told the artist that, unless the artist went back on, he would tell 16,000 of the artist's fans the reason why the concert was being discontinued. Needless to say, in a great huff, the artist decided to go back on.

I've had other near catastrophes. I produced an Alice Cooper concert at the Minneapolis Armory where, on the morning of the show, not only was the portable stage I ordered not constructed, but by accident the stage had been removed from the facility. Fortunately, my production co-ordinator was able to locate a portable stage in nearby St. Paul, and to get permission to use it. That was only part of the problem. One of Alice Cooper's three semivans, which contained all his stage props, had gotten stuck the night be-fore in Chicago. People had already started to assemble out-side the facility at a time when we were thinking seriously about canceling the show. Luckily, at that time I had a Chi-cago office. I called my Chicago man, told him to spend whatever it cost to rent a cargo plane, get that truck to an airport in Chicago, move the equipment onto the plane, and have it flown to Minneapolis for pickup by our local people. Somehow, we did it. The concert went on late, but we averted a riot.

The day of the concert thrusts the concert promoter into a whirlwind of activity. From playing the role of an executive producer, he must now be able to command a small army and cope with myriad emergency problems. It's definitely not a one-man show; without two excellent employees, the production coordinator and the stage manager, the promoter will be up to his neck in arguments, baiting, and fisticuffs. Such responsibility demands a person with exceptional qualities. It also suggests why experienced artists and agents are so careful in their selection of potential concert promoters for major shows.

Preparation is the key to having things go smoothly. Be as organized as you can, with names, telephone numbers, job responsibilities, and delivery times written down clearly. Make a conscious effort to recognize faces, and to know the key people. Be available at all times. If you leave the facility for a half-hour, that's when the trouble is bound to happen. Be flexible, be firm, but also be a diplomat and a philosopher.

Don't speculate about anything, be it large or small. If there's any doubt, find out. But if you're prepared, if you've had a good night's sleep, and if your ticket sales are going smoothly, the day of the concert will be one of the most exhilarating experiences you'll ever have.

13
The Matter of Security

PEOPLE occasionally get hurt going to rock concerts. It is extremely depressing to realize how many charming fifteen- or sixteen-year-old people, whose tickets were paid for by their parents, may not get home without being squashed, bruised, having something thrown on their heads, or worse.

At least five different types of security problems can intrude on an otherwise successful concert performance. The promoter must be prepared to protect the audience from itself, the audience from the police, the police from the audience, the artist and the artist's crew from the audience, and the audience from people who didn't get tickets. This chapter covers some of my personal experiences in the security area, along with tips on how to minimize the risk of something going wrong.

Several weeks before tickets go on sale, the concert promoter should draw up a security plan of action with the head of the facility's in-house security contingent. If the attraction has played at the facility before, it is relatively easy to evaluate whether the security precautions taken for that previous concert were adequate. Security people usually have long memories about concerts that got out of hand. A few minutes on the telephone, or a sit-down meeting with the facility's security head, should help the producer gauge how many city police, private police, and plainclothes security people to use.

If the attraction has never played at the facility, the promoter should contact the attraction's booking agency for information on the attraction's security record at other venues. Here is one instance where the categorizing of rock attractions into punk, acid, hard, middle-of-the-road, and easy-listening groups can be useful. As a rule, heavy metal rock groups will always require more security than the more laid back easy-listening or folk variety. Determining how much security to use can be expressed as a function of the audience's character or personality, which in turn is a function of the artist's music.

Certain security precautions are required by contract. Many facility rental agreements and artist concert riders impose security demands on the promoter. For example: there must be a certain number of men backstage constantly to protect the attraction; there must be one or two men stationed outside the artist's door; there must be a certain number of people who accompany the artist to the stage; the area from the backstage to the stage must be totally enclosed, so that members of the audience cannot get through; only individuals with work, guest, or press passes will be permitted backstage, or at the lip of the stage for photographs; and the promoter must submit to the facility manager in writing, prior to the show, a policy statement on allowing people backstage.

The key to avoiding catastrophe during a rock concert is to show the public a strong, professional sense of organization and control. As the time approaches for placing tickets on sale, the promoter should be in contact with the attraction's agency and the attraction's road manager to decide mutually whether security precautions should be taken at this juncture. This may be the first time for the potential audience to sense whether you, the promoter, are in control of the event, or whether the audience will gain the upper hand. Whenever you anticipate a large turnout of people, you must be prepared. You must put on a positive show of being in charge and able to cope with rowdiness.

Tickets going on sale for groups like The Who or the Rolling Stones almost always mandate a decision on the part of the facility that police barriers be constructed and uniformed police patrol the streets outside the facility. The promoter will be required to pay the cost of these security people and to accept the unilateral declarations of the facility as to the number of internal and external security needed to do the job. Police salaries (for policemen acting as concert security personnel) are usually determined by a policemen's union. Rates vary depending on the rank of the police officer and the time of employment (i.e., regular hours, overtime, holidays). These are predictable costs, not to be overlooked when computing the Total Production Cost on the PCA form.

In cases like this, the mere show of force is usually sufficient to keep the potential audience in line. On an individual basis, however, some crazy things can happen. I was once sued by a young Rolling Stones fan who decided to camp out under a parked car near the facility box office for three days prior to tickets going on sale for a Stones concert in Bloomington, Minnesota. This person literally slept under the parked car for two nights, but on the third morning the owner of the car got in, turned on the ignition, and drove off, right over the Stones fan. Several broken bones were suffered; the Stones fan sued me for negligence, but lost. In reviewing the case, the court felt that it was unusual to take shelter and sleep for two nights under a parked car for the purpose of getting an early Rolling Stones concert ticket.

(These matters are not to be taken lightly. If the situation had been less peculiar, the disposition of the court might have been quite different. Whether the promoter can be insured for incidents that occur weeks prior to a scheduled event, even if they occur outside the facility, is an interesting and presently unresolved point of law.)

The majority of concert attractions will not require a security presence prior to the day of the event. The first major test for nonsuperstar acts is controlling the crowd of ticket and non–ticket holders during the hour or so before the doors of the facility are opened. Quite a number of major attractions have legions of fans who may not be able to get tickets. They may try to crash the concert. They may just want to hang around outside the venue. In my experience, these people represent one of the most frightening aspects of crowd control. Their numbers can easily swell into the thousands. Their energy level is high, and unless properly supervised can lead to ruinous consequences.

Controlling this mob of non–ticket holders is a job for uniformed police. Ideally, they will not brandish sticks or become entrapped in vicious verbal exchanges with bands of young teenagers. They will exude a quiet, nonmilitant professionalism. They will keep people moving around the perimeter of the facility. They will allow only ticket holders for the evening's performance inside their police barriers.

Sometimes it is not possible to attain the ideal security presence. Internal security, which comes along with the facility and is familiar with concert crowds, is more likely to respond to the concert promoter's direction. But external security, which is generally the local city police department, is an autonomous entity, with its own ideas about how security can be effected. It is in the promoter's best interest to play the psychologist with city police. Without their understanding and tolerance of teenage attitudes, and without their respect for you, the promoter, all hell can break loose.

Such was the case in the previously cited Bloomington, Minnesota, concert. The Rolling Stones had sold out the 17,000-seat Metropolitan Sports Center in a matter of hours. I conferred with the police prior to the performance. I urged them to keep kids away from the premises. I told them that the show had already sold out, and that as a result they shouldn't set their barriers right in front of the facility, but blocks away. I urged them not to let anyone near the facility unless he or she had a ticket. I offered these suggestions as an experienced concert promoter, but the city police elected not to take my advice. They didn't set their barriers far enough away from the facility. They let kids come in without tickets. The result was that there were monstrous groups of roving non–ticket holders attempting to break into the facility throughout the evening. They penetrated the police lines, turning over and burning two police cars. The police had to send in gas-masked, mace-throwing troops for their own self-protection. The young cops were scared out of their minds—they had no idea how to cope with the Rolling Stones fans, who had surrounded them. It was a very dangerous situation.

All this was taking place outside the facility. Inside, Mick Jagger began choking in the middle of "Jumping Jack Flash," as one of the mace containers found its way into the ventilating system. Fortunately, most of the audience thought the mace was a clever smoke effect. They remained in their seats. I was ultimately sued for the burned police cars, which were insured. But it never should have happened. It could have been avoided if the city police had been willing to listen to me. Whatever it takes to get on the city police department's wavelength, try your best to become an ally. You need their help, and in turn they may benefit from your guidance. The trick is to find a way to minimize the two or more strikes against you (e.g., youth, long hair, sneakers and blue jeans, stranger in town) and win their respect for you as a professional promoter. Believe me, it's not always easy.

New York City is the only city in my experience that does not allow uniformed cops to moonlight in a security role. The New York City Police Department considers it a conflict of interest for cops to be paid by a second employer to guard a warehouse, for instance, or to pound the pavements outside Madison Square Garden. Personally, I think it's a good policy. It also has some practical benefits for the promoter: it means that, when New York City police are called in for concert duty, the City of New York picks up their tab. The number of city police to be used is determined by the facility manager after he evaluates what type of crowd, and how many young people, a particular rock event is likely to draw. When public safety is being threatened, the New York City Police Department will be in charge of riot control. Their province is outside the facility.

Whenever you see uniformed security inside a hall, they are almost always internal security on the payroll of the facility. This applies not only to New York City, but to virtually every major city in the United States.

I'd like to offer some general observations on how to secure the inside of a concert hall. The primary job of the uniformed internal security is to keep the aisles clear. They will also respond to any calls for help from victimized young people. They look very much like members of the city police, but they're not carrying guns. They're carrying sticks, which can be even more dangerous, since they're used more often.

Uniformed security should not be deployed so that they line the lip of the stage between the audience and the performer. In my opinion, and the opinion of a lot of rock and roll groups, this contradicts the concept of the entertainment event. What I usually do is put uniformed police in the wings and the corners of the facility, so that they have access to the lip of the stage but are hidden from view. If a security force is required in the demilitarized lip area, directly between the performer and the audience, I like it to be young, strong, T-shirted security.

Somehow, the T-shirt seems to be a uniform that everyone can relate to. It doesn't come across as threatening or challenging. My opinion about the men who wear these T-shirts is that they should be big, strong, and ominous. Their presence should be so overwhelming that they discourage most fights from starting.

I normally do not use karate experts to patrol the lip area. I think the 5'7", 135-pound karate expert might have to prove something to a potential aggressor that a 6'5", 250-pound football player would not. It's not important to have the most lethal security force in town. What counts is to discourage acts of aggression from ever happening.

Most major cities have at least one plainclothes security company that provides jobs during the off-season for college football players, basketball players, and other likely part-time security employees. The security personnel you select must believe that it is not their duty to fight. Their job is to try to prevent confrontations, not to "win" when confrontation occurs. If somebody swings at them, they are just supposed to grab the guy in a nondangerous bear hug and get him out of the theater, or turn him over to the police if the guy seems crazy. Only if the aggressor is himself a bear and whacks your guy in the head should there be any retaliation. Fighting should always be the last recourse.

Plainclothes security is cheaper than uniformed police security. Hourly rates range from $2.50 to $5.00, depending on seniority. One of the distinct advantages of working with a plainclothes security company is that the company probably offers workmen's compensation insurance protection to its employees. Trying to assemble your own T-shirted security is not only time consuming, it offers no protection to you, the promoter, if one of your T-shirted security people becomes injured on the job.

I never used uniformed security at the Academy of Music, which seated 3,500 people. Everyone wore T-shirts. I hired ushers, ticket takers, and directors (head ushers) who I felt were capable of helping out with security when needed. No weapons were allowed, not even sticks. For a full house, I used forty people.

At Madison Square Garden I've used anywhere from 200 to 300 internal and plainclothes security people. My Garden security bills often exceeded $4,000 or $5,000. At outdoor venues the cost of security is far, far greater.

Even with 200 or 300 security personnel at Madison Square Garden, you can't breathe easy. Promoters live with the reality that if their sellout audience ever decides to go berserk, the outcome will be decisive. The promoter must lose. If it ever does happen—and it's happened at least once even to the best of professional promoters—roll with the punch. Chalk it up as a loss, but don't let it get you down. Your best protection, of course, is not to let it happen. You must present the appearance of being in firm command of the event. Spread your security around so that they can handle local problems. When you walk through a crowd, walk with confidence. If you talk through the public address system, make it sound as if you own the facility. Half of coming out of a concert clean is simply faking out the audience.

No matter how hard you try, an occasional shocking incident will happen. A cop I know in Atlanta wears a patch over one eye; he lost that eye at a rock concert. One of Peter Frampton's road crew suffered a minor concussion when he was hit on the temple with a bottle thrown from the stands above.

Drug-induced accidents are almost impossible to prevent. I did a show once at the Academy of Music at which a sixteen-year-old girl, with blue warpaint on her face, decided to fly off the mezzanine. She literally took off, landing between the shoulders of two guys who were sitting below in the orchestra. She broke a couple of her ribs on their shoulders, but if she had landed on one of the guy's necks she probably would have killed him. It was a miracle that she, herself, didn't die.

Ironically, the girl's attorney sued me for damages, as though it were my responsibility that she had decided to fly from the mezzanine. In cases like this the promoter must react quickly. Countersue. Put the other party on the defensive. If we hadn't had witnesses, and we hadn't photographed this girl right away with here blue warpaint on, and we hadn't taken her name down, we could have lost the case, absurd as it seems. When accidents do happen, you must move in immediately. Get as many eyewitness accounts as you can. Take plenty of photographs. If you're a good promoter, the burden of proof should tip in your favor. You'll be able to hold negligence suits to a bare minimum, and discourage trial lawyers from taking on a case with you as the defendant.

I've seen a lot of ugliness. I've been in situations where we've had to call other security to protect a cop who was getting beaten up by kids, but refused to use his gun. I've also seen the opposite, with too many cops beating up a kid who could have been handled with a kick in the behind. Much of this brutality, acted out in the present, is actually a retaliation for the beatings cops and audience members received at a previous concert. The key to preventing these incidents from occurring is to build up a respectful relationship between the audience and the police. Each side needs to know the limits beyond which the other side will attack. Each side must be able to bend the law slightly. Each side must cultivate a certain degree of empathy for the other side.

Security is one of the primary reasons that established artists and their agents will not play for novice concert promoters. Some of the really gigantic acts, like Peter Frampton or the Rolling Stones, have learned to go one step further: the facility itself—the four walls, backstage area, and access corridors—must pass a security test. If the facility can't be adequately secured, in the opinion of the supergroup's advance scouts, the act will not play that facility.

The problems of securing an outdoor stadium are immense. I found the uniformed security at Shea Stadium so ineffective (for the purpose of producing concerts) that I had to use every nonuniformed force I could find in New York City for my rock events. I used all my people from the Academy of Music. I used all the people who normally worked the Nassau Coliseum. I used all the people that Ron Delsener used at Shaefer Stadium. I ended up with approximately 500 security people against an audience of 50,000 kids.

Shea Stadium at one time was virgin territory to rock audiences. At the Academy of Music, the kids knew that if they didn't keep the aisles clear, the crazy hippie ushers (my guys) would break their chops. But Shea Stadium was a new place offering virgin challenges. The kids had no idea what they were going to be faced with, and what they were going to be able to get away with. I spent more than $10,000 securing each of my Shea Stadium concerts, but it was always a supreme test. You really must have nerves of steel to promote your dream concert to 50,000 screaming young teenagers.

Please, for the sake of everyone involved, be prepared for that awesome day. Think security. Think adequate insurance protection. It's expensive, it's a nuisance, but it could literally save your life.

14

The Hours after the Concert

THE LAST THING in the world a concert promoter can afford to do is sit back and enjoy his own show. Quite the contrary, the promoter must have hidden reserves of energy and patience to see him through the last few feet of the production gauntlet. Box-office receipts must be reconciled to the satisfaction of the artist's representative, usually the road manager. Confrontations or medical emergencies within the facility must be dealt with. The dismantling of the stage, the unrigging of sound and lights, and the load-out of equipment must be supervised. This chapter covers the remaining areas of responsibility that require the concert promoter's attention.

According to the textbooks, as soon as it appears that the opening act is off to a clean start, the promoter should exit backstage and head for the box office. Here, under the watchful eyes of the artist's representative, the amount of tickets actually sold will be reconciled with the amount of tickets printed, and the artist and facility will be paid. Actually, it doesn't always happen that way. Major facilities, such as Madison Square Garden, will not permit the mad confusion of a rock concert to alter their staid bookkeeping procedures: the promoter and the act will have to wait several weeks for Madison Square Garden to issue accounting statements. Quite a few superstars will trust the promoter to be honest with them on the reconciliation, and to pay them by regular business check rather than in cash. In other cases, where the facility suspects that the show will go OT, or overtime, the facility will insist that settling up occur not during intermission, as is so often required in the artist's concert rider, but at the conclusion of the load-out.

The reconciliation itself is a relatively simple affair. The ticket printer will have provided the promoter a certified statement of the exact number of tickets that were printed for the concert. Against this, the ticket takers will unload their boxes filled with stubs, and a tally will be made of how many tickets were used to attend the concert. If counterfeit tickets are discovered (there shouldn't be any—this is why you have ticket takers), they will be charged against the promoter's potential earnings. Ideally, the number of ticket stubs plus the number of unsold tickets should equal 100 percent of the facility's total seating capacity.

It has become an established practice within the industry for the artist to be able to inspect the promoter's financial records relating to that artist's show for a period of sixty days following the concert. The facility, in turn, will issue financial statements to the promoter that may be challenged over a shorter duration of time (i.e., fifteen to thirty days) if the promoter feels they are incorrect.

Many promoters use the settling-up period to wipe their slate clean of advertising, security, concert rider, and miscellaneous bills incurred for that evening's show. While the reconciliation and bill paying are going on, the promoter must tolerate the presence of the artist's road manager. If the road manager asks for a recount of tickets or money in

front of him, the promoter must oblige. Some road managers can be pretty obnoxious at the settling up, but if your
house is in order and you convey an image of total professionalism, you should get past the reconciliation unscathed.

I've learned from experience to ask the road manager on
the day of the concert how the artist wishes to be paid that
evening, whether in cash or by check. If you go to the trouble of taking $40,000 or $50,000 worth of cash from a bank,
only to have the attraction tell you that they don't need to
go shopping the next day and a check will be all right, you
have the added headache of being responsible for that cash.
Banks will be closed at 12:00 A.M. It's so much money that
I've never felt right, for a variety of reasons, about asking
one of my employees to look after it. Instead, on those occasions when I didn't expect an act to refuse cash, I've had to
spend the night in a hotel room, alone, gnawed by fear that
something might happen. Advance planning should settle
the matter of payment and permit the promoter to enjoy
himself after the show.

In the unfortunate event of a medical emergency, the
promoter should have local listings for an ambulance service, hospital emergency room, and physician included on his
production telephone contact sheet. Large shows today will
almost certainly mandate some form of first-aid staffing at
the facility, but smaller venues may not have the physical
space to accommodate an in-house first-aid room. Make
sure that whoever is in charge of medical emergencies during the concert keeps an accurate account of patient infirmi-
ties and how they are treated, thus avoiding possible open-
ings for lawsuit by audience members who might claim
negligence.

As soon as the concert is completed, the load-out of the at-
traction's sound, stage, and light equipment commences.
Generally, load-outs are much more frantic than load-ins.
The road crew wants literally to get the show on the road.
They may have a long drive to the next facility on the con-

cert tour, and not much time to get there. A major Madison Square Garden production can be dismantled in between two and two and one-half hours, depending on the professionalism of the road crew and on the size of the overall labor force. Many times the promoter will be asked to furnish the act with more stagehands for the load-out than was originally planned. If hiring several more stagehands for postproduction work is clearly a matter of helping the act move on to their next show with time to spare, and if the show just completed went off according to schedule, I'd be pretty insistent that the act, rather than the promoter, pay for those additional stagehands.

Normally, I've relied on my production coordinator to supervise the load-out from the facility. My postconcert time is spent either settling up in the box office or attending one or more afterconcert parties thrown by the act's record company, agency, management, or the act itself. Parties are not just for having fun: they're important political opportunities to get ahead with the act and the agency, provided the show was a triumph. All the participants will pretend they have nothing on their minds, but business is never far below the surface among concert people.

My party psychology is never to take the initiative, but to be available to talk with the agent, spend more time with the personal manager, be gracious with the record company executives, and congratulate the act on a superb concert. If it really was a sensational concert, and you had something to do with its success, you're in line for more shows, more acts, more profits. But let the agency come to you, for a change. You'll discover what a heady feeling that can be.

15

The Choice

IN THESE PAGES I've attempted to portray the industry in realistic terms, spreading before the reader a detailed canvas of cause and effect, positive features and negative drawbacks. Before we part company, I would like to make some final comments, not only about the future of concert promotion but about the manner in which I've written this book.

Concert promotion can never be expressed as a science. The narrative style I've used—describing each element of the business, using actual illustrations wherever possible, then moving on—was chosen not out of the desire to be brief, but because I don't think there is any other way to write effectively about concert promotion as a serious subject. Some readers, of course, might dispute this. Certainly there may be some oversights here that will be corrected in future editions. But I would vigorously oppose any attempt to make concert promotion more malleable to long-term study, first because it's really not that complicated on paper, and second because textbook learning is a poor substitute for empirical knowledge. The best way not only to learn concert promotion, but to discover whether you have the aptitude to survive in this highly competitive industry, is through firsthand experience.

Where concert promotion does become a difficult subject is in the living world: the three-dimensional clashing of antagonistic forces, superior intellects, and unforeseen circumstances. The value to you in reading this book should be, "Take this knowledge and run with it." Learn to think before you open your mouth. Learn how to plan—so many mistakes will be avoided if only you plan, plan, plan, down to the most minute production molecule. Bring this added intelligence and capacity for planning with you when you begin contacting facilities, agents, clubs, and record companies. Not only will it help you obtain professional results—it will point up some of the critical dangers of aspiring to be a concert promoter in the 1980s.

As you begin making the rounds, the horrible truths will begin hitting home. In New York City, the most densely populated metropolitan area in the United States, there is virtually no chance today of becoming a major concert promoter. The story is the same in Los Angeles, Chicago, Denver, Miami, and Nashville. The opportunity existed fifteen years ago. The relationships were developed, tested, and cemented ten years ago. If one of the principal promoters were to die suddenly, his son or daughter might take over, or the facility manager's son or daughter might take over, or the agent's son or daughter might take over, or some other trusted member of the inner circle would be tried first, before any outside prospects were allowed in. As for the smaller U.S. cities, they will be eyed increasingly by young promoters who have already paid their dues at clubs and are solidifying relationships with the best facilities in these smaller towns. Where are you, the outsider looking in, realistically going to penetrate this business?

Another question, stated even more bluntly: does it make sense financially to desire a career as a professional rock concert promoter? I've tried to be impartial in my description of how promoters negotiate talent and facility fees. But the true condition of this business does not augur well for the promoter. It is a seller's market deluxe. Service to the agency is essential. Developing the agency's start-up attractions, who can't possibly make money unless they're playing in major clubs, will be a constant drain on the promoter's finances throughout his career. There is no guarantee that the agency will permit you to promote bigger acts. When you do begin producing larger shows, your profit potential will be restricted. You will discover in a hundred different ways how unimportant you are to the agency, the attraction, and the road manager. And what happens if you complain? Expulsion from the industry. Blacklisting. Bankruptcy. Is it worth it?

In order to become a successful concert promoter you will have to become a master strategist, budget planner, production coordinator, advertiser, publicist, diplomat, advisor to artists, and honest businessman. In other areas of the multi-billion dollar music industry, these skills command salaries and job security that are virtually nonexistent in the concert promotion field. Working for a record company, you might actually get home several nights a week and see your family. The pressure isn't as great. You're a member of a team. You'll be able to make friends within the company and friends within the industry. You won't be "that upstart young promoter" who is constantly asking favors. You'll have taken your skills and transferred them to another part of the music business. In return, you'll be treated with something the promotion industry may never give you: respect.

I could go on and on offering intelligent arguments against becoming a rock concert promoter. And yet, if the promoting instinct is in your blood, you will be compelled at least to give concert promotion a try. That's fine. But be reasonable. Recognize what you're up against. Know that every place you go today, the competition will be intense and money will be tight. Never before has this business required so much ingenuity on the part of individual concert promoters merely to survive.

Frankly, I don't think the market can support many more conventional rock and roll concert promoters. The key, then, is to be unconventional. That means, for my money, be eminently practical. Study the music business as you've never studied it before. Go to clubs, read the trades, talk to people, get out and dance—try to discover what's really happening in your town that involves music, entertainment, and large profits.

Follow that lead. Have some kind of focus when you approach an agent. Be able to specify to the loan officer of the bank the ways in which you're planning to utilize your club. Think dollars and cents, not flashy names and Cadillac limousines. See if you can construct a business on paper that will exist far into the future: three years, five years, seven years from today. This elementary kind of business planning, so alien to the rock and roll concert promotion industry, is the key to spotting new opportunities, capitalizing on those opportunities, and moving ahead.

The field that I think is most worthy of exploration involves ways in which the methodology and love of promoting concerts can be allied to other, more financially productive areas of the music business. Research and development of new ideas will be necessary. An apprenticeship in the concert promotion business might be essential. But the end result may be a way to beat the odds, get out from under the thumb of agents, artists, and contract riders, and become, in every sense of the word, a free person. That, coupled with the sheer joy of promoting concerts, would make a career in this fascinating corner of the music industry still worthwhile and personally fulfilling.

Appendix A
The Six Largest Rock Booking Agencies

(In Alphabetical Order)

American Talent International Ltd.
(ATI)
888 Seventh Avenue
New York, N.Y. 10019
212-977-2300
Other office in Beverly Hills, Calif.

International Creative Management
(ICM)
40 West 57 Street
New York, N.Y. 10019
212-586-0440
Other offices in Los Angeles,
Las Vegas, Miami, London,
Paris, Rome

Magna Artists Corp.
1370 Avenue of the Americas
New York, N.Y. 10019
212-489-8027
Other office in Los Angeles

Monterey Peninsula Artists
P.O. Box 7308
Carmel, California 93921
408-624-4889

William Morris Agency
1350 Avenue of the Americas
New York, N.Y. 10019
212-586-5100
Other offices in Chicago, Beverly Hills,
Nashville, London

Premier Talent
3 East 54 Street
New York, N.Y. 10022
212-758-4900

Appendix B
Production Cost Analysis Form

Attraction _____
Support _____
Place _____
Date _____
Time _____
Weather _____
Seating Capacity _____
Ticket Prices _____
Gross Potential _____
  Less Taxes _____
GP Less Taxes _____

	Budget	Advanced	Actual	Variance
Talent				
Headliner—Guarantee				
Headliner—PC				
Support—Guarantee				
Support—PC				
Opening Act—Guarantee/Bonus				
Third Act—Guarantee/Bonus				
Fourth Act—Guarantee/Bonus				
Local Musicians				
Other				

	Budget	Advanced	Actual	Variance
Tickets				
Printing				
Ticketron				
Distribution				
Other				
Facility				
Rental—Guarantee				
Rental—PC				
House Manager				
Assistant House Manager				
Company Manager				
General Manager				
Ushers				
Directors				
Ticket Takers				
Internal Security				
External Security				
Police Department				
Electricity/Heat				
Air Conditioning				
Water/Sewerage				
Other				
Box Office				
Treasurer				
Assistant Treasurer				
Ticket Sellers				
Telephone Person				
Telephone Bill				
Stamps and Envelopes				
Other				
Maintenance				
Janitor				
Porters				

	Budget	Advanced	Actual	Variance
Maintenance				
Valets				
Matrons				
Exterminator				
Holmes Security				
Cartage				
Supplies				
Repairs				
Upkeep				
Engineers and Handymen				
Other				
Production				
Stage Construction				
Seat Construction				
Spotlight Rental Fee				
Fork Lift				
Scaffolding				
TV Projectors				
Video Screens				
Cables				
Sound				
Lights				
Curtains and Backdrop				
Other				
Production Personnel				
Stagehands				
Electricians				
Spotlight Operators				
Production Coordinator				
Stage Manager				

	Budget	Advanced	Actual	Variance
Production Personnel				
Assistant Stage Manager				
Teamsters				
Other				
Headline Rider				
Limousines				
Piano				
Organ				
Tuner				
Refreshments				
Hostess				
Trucks/Vans				
Trailer				
Cranes				
Telephone				
Other				
Support Rider				
Limousines				
Piano				
Organ				
Tuner				
Refreshments				
Hostess				
Trucks/Vans				
Trailer				
Cranes				
Telephone				
Other				

	Budget	Advanced	Actual	Variance
Insurance				
Personal Liability				
Property Damage				
Fire				
Building Damage				
Stick-up				
Other				
Legal				
Accounting				
ASCAP/BMI/SESAC				
Producer's Direct				
Concert Expense				
Transportation				
Hotel				
Other				
Production Coordinator's Direct				
Concert Expense				
Transportation				
Hotel				
Other				
Advertising and Promotion				
Radio				
Television				
Publications				

	Budget	Advanced	Actual	Variance
Advertising and Promotion PR				
Production				
Signs				
Posters				
Flyers				
Marquee				
Other				
First Aid Doctors				
Nurses				
Ambulances				
Overtime				
Sunday Premium				
Gratuities 1.				
2.				
3.				
Total Costs				
Audience Break-Even				
Actual Gross Less Taxes				
Gross Profit				

Appendix C
Major Facility License Agreement

AGREEMENT made   ,   between   , a corporation (Licensor), and Towne House Concerts, Ltd. (Licensee).

1. **License.** Licensor hereby grants to Licensee the license and privilege (the License) to use the area or areas (the Premises) designated as the Arena, excepting Loges Nos. 11C (Rows A,B,C), 15A (Row B, Seats 1–2; Row C, Seats 1–4), 15B (Rows A,B), 39C (Row C) and 47C (Rows A,B), plus 58 additional seats to be selected by Licensor for its own use or the use of its designees to be returned to the Box Office prior to the Event for sale if not used in   (the Building) for a period (the Period commencing at 8:00 A. M. on   and ending at 1:00 A. M. on   for the sole purpose of presenting an entertainment program featuring   (the Event).

2. **Utilization of Period.** The Period shall be utilized by Licensee as follows:

8:00 A. M.–12:00 Noon	Move In
1:00 P. M.– 5:00 P. M.	Rehearsal
8:00 P. M.–10:30 P. M.	Performance
10:31 P. M.– 1:00 A. M.	Move Out

3. **Compensation.** In consideration of the grant of the License by Licensor to Licensee and the use of the Premises as provided herein, Licensee agrees to pay to Licensor, without demand: A. $27,500 payable as follows: (a) $9,500 payable upon execution hereof; (b) $9,000 payable on or before   ; and (c) $9,000

139

payable on or before   ; plus B. 22 1/2% of Net Gate Receipts in
excess of $130,000 payable on   . The term "Net Gate Receipts" as
used herein shall mean the entire proceeds from the sale of tickets of admission to
the Event, less Federal, state and local taxes, including gross receipts and admission
taxes. In addition, Licensee agrees to pay to Licensor the sum of $27,500 payable
on or before   to cover estimated charges for personnel, services,
equipment and materials furnished by Licensor to Licensee in accordance with
Paragraph 6 hereof. In   the event actual expenses incurred pursuant
to Paragraph 6 hereof are in excess of or less than $27,500, the payment hereunder
shall be adjusted and payment shall be made therefor pursuant to Paragraph
22 of the Standard Terms and Conditions attached hereto and made a part hereof.

4. **Sources of Licensee's Income.** Licensee represents and warrants to Licensor
that neither Licensee nor any parent, subsidiary, partner, co-venturer, associate or
affiliate of Licensee shall derive any revenue, income or compensation from the
Event from any source or by any means whatsoever except:

Licensee's share of Net Gate Receipts from the sale of tickets of admission to
the Event.

5. **Standard Terms and Conditions.** Attached hereto are the Licensor's Standard Terms and Conditions. All of the terms and conditions set forth in such Standard Terms and Conditions are incorporated in this Agreement by reference as fully as though set forth at length in this Agreement. Licensee acknowledges that it has
read such Standard Terms and Conditions.

6. **Personnel, Services, etc.** Licensee shall employ, and Licensor may at its option designate or furnish, the following personnel, services, equipment and
materials pursuant to the terms and conditions contained herein:

(a) Licensor's special police, in a number sufficient in Licensor's opinion,
which shall be conclusive, adequately to police the Premises and other portions of
the Building inside and out affected by Licensee's use thereof.

(b) A sufficient number of ticket sellers, ticket takers, doormen, ushers, maids,
porters, watchmen and other special force personnel.

(c) Such telephone service as Licensee may request, to be paid for at legal rates
and furnished at Licensor's option to Licensee through Licensor's switchboard.

(d) Ticket printing.

(e) All plumbing, carpentry and electrical work or other services and all gas or
other materials required to fit the Premises for the use of Licensee or its exhibitors,
if any.

(f) Selling commissions to Ticketron, Inc.

All personnel, services, equipment and materials furnished Licensee by Licensor,
whether pursuant to the provisions of this Agreement, any agreement supplementing this Agreement, any work order, or otherwise, shall, unless otherwise provided
in this Agreement be paid for by Licensee, at such rates as may be specified in this
Agreement, or any agreement supplementing this Agreement, or the provisions of
any work order, and if no such rates shall be specified at the cost to Licensor or the

prevailing rate of wages (including full reimbursement for Licensor's fringe benefit and payroll tax expenses in connection with the Event), plus an additional 10% for supervision and overhead. Any charges for any personnel, services, material or equipment furnished by Licensor to Licensee which are payable by Licensee shall become due and payable when the same are furnished, and payment therefor shall be made as provided in paragraph 23 of the Standard Terms and Conditions attached hereto.

The Rider attached hereto containing paragraph(s) 8–24 is hereby made a part hereof.

IN WITNESS WHEREOF Licensor and Licensee have caused this Agreement to be executed the day and year first above written.

LICENSOR

LICENSEE
TOWNE HOUSE CONCERTS, LTD.

Name of Licensee

Address of Licensee

By   By
   Name   Title   Name   Title

7. Notwithstanding Paragraph 22 of the Standard Terms and Conditions attached hereto, Licensor consents to Licensee's use of the name of the Building, provided that such name is used only for the purpose of advising persons attending the Event where the Event is to be held. Licensee agrees to submit copies of any such proposed use to Licensor for Licensor's approval as to accuracy. Should any further use of the name be intended, Licensee will submit copies of the proposed use to Licensor in advance for Licensor's approval.

8. With respect to any or all services, whether furnished by Licensor to Licensee with or without charge, or whether furnished by Licensee, Licensor shall in no event by liable for a failure to provide such services, or for the acts or omissions of any person or persons with respect to such services due to strikes, labor disputes, accidents or causes beyond the control or prevention of Licensor.

Idemnification and Insurance

9. **Indemnification:** Licensee hereby agrees to indemnify and hold harmless Licensor against any and all claims whatsoever (including court costs and attorneys' fees and related disbursements) caused by or alleged to have been caused by any act or omission to act of Licensee, its officers, employees, servants, or agents or any artist appearing in the Event (including artists' support personnel) in connection with the presentation of the Event.

9-1. During the term hereof, Licensee shall keep in effect, with insurance companies licensed to do business in   and with a minimum of an "A" rating in Best's Insurance Guide, the following insurance naming Licensor, et al., as additional insured (excepting Workmen's Compensation Insurance) therein:

(a) *Public Liability Insurance*

    (1) Bodily Injury Coverage which covers Licensor and Licensee, each of their officers, employees, servants and agents and which provides for limits of liability of at least $1,000,000 for personal injuries to (as defined in Exhibit "A" hereto) or the death of one or more persons in any occurrence caused or alleged to have been caused by any act or omission to act by any artist appearing in the Event or by Licensee or its officers, employees, servants, and agents in connection with the presentation of the Event.

    (2) Property Damage Coverage which covers Licensor and Licensee and each of their officers, employees, servants and agents and which provides for limits of liability of at least $100,000 for property damage in any one occurrence caused by or alleged to have been caused by any act or omission to act by any of the artists appearing in the Event or by Licensee or its officers, employees, servants or agents in connection with the presentation of the Event.

    (3) Fire Legal Liability Coverage which provides coverage to Licensor and which provides a limit of liability of $100,000 for any one occurrence, with a deductible not to exceed $1,000 for damage to the property of Licensor caused by or alleged to have been caused by any of the artists appearing in the Event or by Licensee or its officers, employees, servants or agents in connection with the presentation of the Event.

(b) *Other Insurance*

Workmen's Compensation Insurance, Employers Liability Insurance and all other insurance coverage of similar character applicable or relating to the employment of Licensee's officers, employees, servants, agents or independent contractors.

9-2. Licensee hereby agrees to indemnify and hold Licensor harmless for any damage to the property of the Licensor, up to $50,000, caused by any act or omission to act by any artist (including artists support personnel) appearing in the Event or by Licensee or its officers, employees, servants and agents in connection with the presentation of the Event. This indemnification shall be covered by insurance and the certificates of insurance evidencing this coverage, with a deductible not to exceed $5,000, shall make specific reference to the foregoing indemnification.

9-3. Licensee hereby agrees to indemnify Licensor for any damage to the property of the Licensor caused by persons attending the Event. All repairs to the damaged property of Licensor shall be made by the firm(s) designated by Licensor. The charges for services by said firm(s) shall not exceed the charges generally prevailing for comparable services.

The certificates of insurance certifying to the issuance and existence of said policies shall be delivered to Licensor at least thirty (30) days prior to the date of the Event. In the event that said certificates are not received by the date required, Licensor, at the sole cost and expense of Licensee, shall have the right to purchase the Public Liability and Indemnification Insurance to protect the interests of Licensor, et al. Licensor's failure to purchase said insurance coverage shall not give rise to any claim by Licensee against Licensor, and shall not relieve Licensee of any of its obligations under this Agreement.

10. Licensee agrees that it will contract for all musicians, other than self- contained units, to be used in connection with the Event, (including auxiliary and additional musicians) through Licensor.

11. Licensee agrees to reimburse Licensor for (a) any fees paid to ASCAP, BMI, SESAC and any similar organization for the use of music in the Event, and (b) additional musicians, if any, required for the Event.

12. All advertising, including newspaper advertising and promotional releases are to be submitted for approval by Licensor at least seven (7) days prior to its intended publication. Under no circumstances will advertising which combines ads for events to be held at the Building with ads for any other location be permitted or approved. In all printed advertising, including newspapers, the standard Licensor logo or other logo designated by Licensor, must be displayed and positioned in the manner selected by Licensor in the sole exercise of its discretion. In the event Licensee fails to comply with the requirements of this Paragraph 12, Licensor will suffer damages as a result thereof. Due to the difficulty in ascertaining such damages, Licensee agrees to pay to Licensor the sum of $5,000 as liquidated damages in the event of such failure to comply. Payment of said $5,000 shall be made pursuant to Paragraph 22 of the Standard Terms and Conditions.

13. Licensee shall submit to Licensor at least two (2) weeks prior to the Event a list of all persons to appear in the Event, the appearances of such persons to be subject to Licensor's prior approval, such approval not to be unreasonably withheld.

14. Licensee agrees to pay to Licensor the sum of $5,000 as liquidated damages, for each performance during which any person appearing in the Event encourages vocally or by hand or body movement, members of the audience to leave their seats. Licensor may retain any monies due to Licensee pursuant to Paragraph 22 of the Standard Terms and Conditions to offset any such sums that may be due to Licensor pursuant to this Paragraph. The foregoing shall not impair or diminish Licensor's rights to recover such larger damages as Licensor may suffer and prove, or limit or restrict any other legal or equitable remedy available to Licensor due to the actions of Licensee or any of the persons appearing in the Event. In addition, Licensee agrees that no person appearing in the Event will use obscene language or gestures during their appearance subject to the same liquidated damages set forth above.

15. Ticket scale as determined by Licensee shall be $7.50, $6.50 and $5.50 with the house grossed to approximately $133,000.

16. Licensee agrees to use the services of Ticketron, Inc. for the sale of tickets to the Event.

17. Licensor reserves the right to:

(a) assign working-area perimeters for all photographic coverage of the Event by working press including newspaper, magazine, wire service and related personnel and to restrict the amount of such personnel which may be accommodated at the Event;

(b) permit photographic coverage by such media which, in its judgment, should be allowed such access irrespective of any other consideration;

(c) review upon demand the seat allocation for all reporters, critics, reviewers and other working press personnel which have been made by any designated representative of the Event;

(d) allocate seat locations for working press personnel which may have been denied such accreditation (upon formal application) by any designated representative of the Event. The allocation shall consist of up to ten (10) prime seat locations or ten percent (10%) of the agreed-upon press allocation, whichever is greater, and further, to hold such locations in its box office until twenty-four (24) hours prior to the starting time of the Event for utilization for said purpose. If not used for the accommodation of media representatives, such seat locations so held will be released for sale with revenues from such sales to be divided in accordance with the terms of this Agreement;

(e) accredit and assign locations for all newsfilm coverage of the Event, expressly providing for a two-minute limitation upon the use of such film footage as may be taken for general news purposes;

(f) require a declaration, in writing, on the part of the Licensee as to the policy it wishes to establish with respect to entrance into areas generally considered to be "back-stage" and/or dressing room areas by working press personnel; and further require that this declaration be made not later than seventy-two (72) hours prior to the starting time of the Event. Licensor shall take what steps it considers appropriate to inform legitimate media representatives of such policy;

(g) require distinctive and visual identification of working press personnel such as are to be admitted to said areas by means of a credential which shall be approved by Licensor not later than twenty-four (24) hours prior to the starting time of the Event;

(h) inform its security personnel to enforce fully all of the foregoing; and

(i) inform the designated press representative of the Event of the above requirements and require that said representative be designated not later than seven (7) days prior to the Event.

18. Licensor retains the right to sell, on a seasonal basis, boxes designated as The Hall of Fame Lounge Boxes specially constructed in Licensor's facility above

the mezzanine level. All proceeds from the sale of such boxes shall belong exclusively to Licensor.

19. Licensor reserves the right to sell seats to the Event in the Portal Boxes to its designees, such sales to be made at $7.50 per seat and the proceeds from said sales shall be paid to Licensee by Licensor pursuant to Paragraph 22 of the Standard Terms and Conditions. In the event that Licensor does not sell any or all such seats at least seven (7) days prior to the Event, such seats shall then be made available to Licensee for its sale.

20. Licensee represents and warrants that all laser devices to be operated in connection with the presentation of the Event, if any, shall be adequately registered with the Commissioner of the   and that the operator(s) thereof shall have an appropriate Certificate of Competence issued by the   . Documentation verifying the foregoing shall be submitted to the Licensor prior to the presentation of the Event. Licensee further certifies that the operation of laser devices during the presentation of the Event shall be in full compliance with Industrial Code   of   and all other applicable Federal, state and local directives. Notwithstanding the foregoing, Licensee shall not use any laser devices whatsoever during the presentation of the Event without the prior written consent of the Licensor.

21. Licensee represents and warrants that it has been authorized by the artists advertised by Licensee to appear in the Event to enter into this Agreement relating to such appearance and that Licensee has the rights to guarantee the artist's appearance pursuant to this Agreement.

22. Licensee represents and warrants that all welding relating to trusses or comparable fixtures to be utilized by the Licensee during the Event has been or shall be performed or supervised by a licensed or comparably state-qualified welder. All of such welding shall be subject to the approval of Licensor, which shall not be unreasonably withheld.

23. Licensor shall admit no more than fifty (50) non-working persons to the back stage area of the Premises at any one time during the Period.

EXHIBIT "A"

Definition of "Personal Injury"

The term "Personal Injury" as used in the Agreement shall include bodily injury, plus injury arising out of the following groups of offenses:
   A. False arrest, detention or imprisonment, or malicious prosecution.
   B. Libel, slander, defamation or violation of right of privacy.
   C. Wrongful entry or eviction or other invasion of right of private occupancy.

LICENSE AGREEMENT STANDARD TERMS AND CONDITIONS

1. Definitions. When used herein, "this Agreement" shall mean the Agreement to which these Standard Terms and Conditions are attached and shall include such Standard Terms and Conditions, and the terms "Licensor", "Licensee", "the Premises", "the Building", "the Period" and "the Event" shall have the same meanings as set forth in the Agreement to which these Standard Terms and Conditions are attached.

2. No Representations by Licensor. Neither Licensor nor Licensor's employees or agents have made any representations or promises with respect to the Premises, and Licensee has examined the Premises and is satisfied with the condition, fitness and order thereof. Commencement of the use of the Premises by Licensee shall be conclusive evidence against Licensee that the Premises were in good repair and in satisfactory condition, fitness and order when such use commenced.

3. Assignment. Licensee shall not assign or encumber this Agreement and shall not permit the Premises or any part thereof to be used or occupied by others without the prior written consent of Licensor. If this Agreement is assigned or if the Premises or any part thereof are used or occupied by anyone other than Licensee, Licensor may collect compensation from the assignee, user or occupant and apply the net amount collected to the amount payable by Licensee to Licensor hereunder, but no such assignment, use, occupancy, or collection shall be deemed a waiver of Licensee's obligations hereunder, the acceptance of the assignee, user or occupant as a licensee or tenant, or a release of Licensee from its obligations hereunder.

4. Requirements of Law, Fire Insurance, etc. Licensee shall comply with the requirements of all laws, orders and regulations of Federal, state, county and municipal authorities and with any lawful direction of public officers which shall impose any duty upon Licensor or Licensee with respect to the Premises or the use and occupancy thereof. Licensee shall comply with all the rules, orders, regulations or requirements of the Board of Fire Underwriters or any other similar body and shall not do or permit anything to be done in or about the Premises or the Building or bring or keep anything therein which shall increase the rate of fire insurance on the Building or on property located therein, except as permitted by the Fire Department, Board of Fire Underwriters, Fire Insurance Rating Organization or any other authority having jurisdiction. No gasoline, acetylene or other fuel or combustible will be admitted to the Building without the approval of Licensor and the Bureau of Combustibles of the Fire Department. Any decorating or other work, and the material therefor, done or furnished by Licensee shall be subject to approval by Licensor and the Fire Department and, unless so approved may be prevented or removed by Licensor. No moving picture machine shall be permitted in the Building unless the same shall first have been approved by and a certificate procured from the Electrical Bureau of the Department of Water Supply, Gas and Electricity, the Fire Department or any other department of having jurisdiction over the use or operation thereof.

5. Alterations, Signs, etc. Licensee shall not mark, paint, drill into or in any way mar or deface any part of the Premises or the Building. Licensee shall not display or erect any lettering, signs, pictures, notices or advertisements upon any part of the outside or inside of the Building or make any alterations or improvements in or to the Premises or the Building without the prior written consent of Licensor.

6. Entrances, Watchmen, etc. The entrances and exits of the Premises shall be locked or unlocked as Licensee may direct, subject to regulations of Federal, state, county and municipal authorities, to any lawful direction of public officers, and to Licensor's approval. Licensee shall at its expense at all times maintain watchmen designated by Licensor at all exits and entrances when such exits and entrances are unlocked. Articles, fittings, fixtures, materials and equipment shall be brought into or removed from the Building only at entrances and exits designated by Licensor. No vehicle which with its contents weights more than 15 tons shall be permitted by Licensee to enter the Building without the prior written consent of Licensor.

7. Use of Services and Facilities. Licensee acknowledges that besides the use of the Premises as contemplated by this Agreement, the Building and various parts thereof and areas therein may or will be used for the installation, holding or presentation, and removal of activities, events and engagements other than the Event, and that in order for the Building to operate as efficiently as practicable it may or will be necessary for the use or availability of services and facilities of the Building, including without limitation entrances, exits, truck ramps, receiving areas, marshalling areas, storage areas, passenger and freight elevators and concession areas, to be scheduled or shared. Licensee agrees that Licensor shall have full, complete and absolute authority to establish the schedules for the use and availability of such services and facilities and to determine when and the extent to which the sharing of any such services and facilities is necessary or desirable, and Licensee agrees to comply with any schedules so established and to cooperate in any sharing arrangements so determined.

8. Removal of Disorderly Persons, etc. Licensee hereby appoints Licensor, or any servant, employee or agent of Licensor, Licensee's agent to refuse admission to or cause to be removed from the Premises or the Building any undesirable person. Any artisans or workmen employed by Licensee shall be under the general supervision and control of Licensor (but not as an agent or servant of Licensor) while on the Premises or in the Building and may be refused entrance to or ejected from the Premises and the Building by Licensor for non-compliance with any provision of this Agreement or for objectionable or improper conduct without any liability on Licensor's part for such refusal or ejectment. No collections, whether for charity or otherwise, shall be made or attempted without the prior written consent of Licensor.

9. Rules and Regulations. Licensee shall, and shall cause its servants, agents, employees, licensees, patrons and guests to, abide by such reasonable rules and regulations as may from time to time be adopted by Licensor for the use, occupancy and operation of the Premises and the Building.

10. Destruction, Fire, etc. If the Premises or any other portion of the Building is destroyed prior to or during the Period to an extent that, in Licensor's opinion, which shall be conclusive, the Premises cannot be used by Licensee as provided herein, this Agreement shall cease and terminate, in which event the amounts payable by Licensee to Licensor under the paragraph in this Agreement headed "Compensation" shall be pro-rated to the time of such cessation and termination and shall be paid by Licensee to Licensor. Unless this Agreement so ceases and terminates, there shall be no abatement of the amounts payable by Licensee to Licensor hereunder. Licensee hereby waives and releases Licensor from all damages, compensation or claims for damages to any person or property caused by such destruction, whether or not this Agreement so ceases and terminates.

11. End of Period, etc. Upon the expiration of the Period or the termination of this Agreement for any reason whatsoever prior to the expiration of the Period, Licensee shall immediately quit and surrender the Premises to Licensor. Upon such quitting and surrender, the Premises shall, subject to the performance by Licensor of its obligations under paragraph 5 of these Standard Terms and Conditions, be in the same condition of cleanliness as at the beginning of the period and in good order, ordinary wear and damage by the elements excepted. Licensee shall remove from the Premises and the Building any goods or chattels brought or permitted by it on the Premises and in the Building. For non-compliance with the provisions of this paragraph, Licensee shall pay to Licensor as liquidated damages for each day or portion thereof during which the Premises are not surrendered or such goods or chattels are not removed a sum equal to three times the amount equal to the daily average amount paid and payable by Licensee to Licensor under the paragraph in this Agreement headed "Compensation", which daily average amount shall be computed on the basis of the aggregate amount paid and payable by Licensee to Licensor under such paragraph headed "Compensation" and the number of days or pro rata part thereof that Licensee was entitled to use the Premises hereunder.

12. Indemnification, Insurance, etc. Licensee agrees to protect, indemnify and hold harmless Licensor from any and all liability, damage or expense for, upon or by reasons of (i) any injury or injuries, including injuries resulting in death, received by any person, firm or corporation to his or its person or his or its property and (ii) any loss of property received, done or occurring in or about the Premises, the entrances, lobbies and exits thereof, the sidewalks, streets and approaches adjoining the Building, or any portion of the Building used by Licensee hereunder, unless resulting from negligence of Licensor or its servants, employees or agents in the operation or maintenance of the Premises or the Building. Without limiting the generality of the foregoing, Licensee agrees to pay all costs and expenses of the defense and settlement, including any amount in settlement, of any and all claims and actions at law or in equity which may be asserted or brought against Licensor because of any such injuries, damage or loss, even though such claims or actions may be groundless, false or fraudulent, to permit Licensor to supervise the defense to or settlement of any such claim or action, and to pay and discharge any judgments, orders or decrees rendered or entered against Licensor by reason thereof.

13. Concessions. Licensor reserves and retains to itself and its assignees, licensees and designees the privilege of using such parts of the Premises as in its opinion, which shall be conclusive, are necessary or desirable for or to the operation of all concessions in the Premises and in the Building, including without limitation the concessions of checking clothing and other personal property and the sale of drinks, food, tobacco products, programs and souvenirs, which concessions are reserved and retained by Licensor for the benefit of itself or its assignees, licensees or designees. No charge for the checking of clothing or other personal property shall be included in or added to the general admission price, if any, for the Event.

14. Access and Announcements. Licensor, its officers, directors, servants, employees, agents, concessionaires, and its concessionaires' servants, employees and agents shall at all times have free access to the Premises upon presentation of usual passes issued to them by Licensor. Licensor, at such reasonable time or times as it may deem appropriate, may announce, describe and advertise over the sound system in the Premises, including without limitation announcements, descriptions and advertisements concerning other or future events being or to be held in the Premises, in other parts of the Building or elsewhere.

15. Air Conditioning and Light. Licensor shall furnish air conditioning, including heat and air cooling, to the Premises with the permanent equipment with which the Building is equipped at such times and in such amounts as shall be reasonably necessary in Licensor's opinion, which shall be conclusive, for the comfortable use and occupancy of the Premises and shall furnish illumination to the Premises at reasonable hours with the permanent equipment (not including spotlights) with which the Premises are equipped, except when prevented by strikes, accidents or other causes beyond the control or prevention of Licensor and except during the repairing of equipment and apparatus in the Building which is provided for such air conditioning and illuminating purposes.

16. Default. (a) If before or during the Period (i) Licensee makes a general assignment for the benefit of creditors or takes the benefit of any insolvency act, (ii) a receiver or trustee is appointed for Licensee or Licensee's property, (iii) execution is issued pursuant to a judgment rendered against Licensee, (iv) this Agreement is assigned, passed to or desolves upon any person, firm or corporation other than Licensee or Licensee attempts to assign this Agreement without the prior written consent of Licensor, (v) use of the Premises for the purpose of any of the purposes specified under the paragraph in this Agreement headed "License" is forbidden or temporarily suspended by competent public authority, (vi) Licensee defaults in the performance or observance of any of its obligations or agreements contained herein, including the agreement to make payments as provided herein, or (vii) Licensee vacates or deserts the Premises (in which case surrender of the keys shall not be necessary to constitute vacation or desertion), then, in any such event, this Agreement shall, at Licensor's option expressed in a 12-hour written notice to Licensee, expire as fully and completely as if such date and time of expiration were the date and time definitely fixed herein for the expiration of the Period and of this Agreement, and Licensee shall then quit and surrender the Premises to Licensor, but Licensee shall remain liable as herinafter provided.

(b) Licensor or any other person by its order may immediately upon the expiration of this Agreement as provided in subparagraph (a) above, or at any time thereafter, enter the Premises and remove all persons and all or any property therefrom by summary dispossess proceedings, or by any suitable action or proceeding at law, or by force or otherwise, without being liable to indictment, prosecution or damages therefor, and possess and enjoy the Premises together with all additions, alterations and improvements. In any case where pursuant to the provisions of this Agreement or by summary proceedings or otherwise this Agreement expires or is terminated before the date and time definitely fixed herein for the expiration of the Period and this Agreement, and in all cases of entry by Licensor, Licensor may, but shall not be required to, relicense or let the Premises or any part or parts thereof, as the agent of Licensee or otherwise, at any time or times during the Period, for whatever compensation or rent Licensor shall obtain, and Licensee shall, whether or not the Premises are relicensed or let, be and remain liable for, and Licensee hereby agrees to pay to Licensor as damages, an amount equal to all amounts payable by Licensee to Licensor hereunder, less the amount thereof already paid and the net avails of relicensing or letting, if any, remaining after deducting the expenses which Licensor may have incurred in entering and relicensing or letting, and the same shall be due and payable by Licensee to Licensor at the times specified herein for payments by Licensee to Licensor hereunder. Licensee hereby expressly waives (i) the service of notice of intention to enter and any and all right of redemption, (ii) to the extent permitted by law, the service of the 10-day notice to quit provided for in

, and (iii) all rights to trial by jury in any proceedings hereafter instituted by Licensor against Licensee in respect to the Premises or this Agreement. Licensee also agrees that if Licensor commences any summary dispossess proceeding against Licensee, Licensee shall not interpose any counterclaim of whatever nature or description in any such proceeding.

(c) In the event of a breach or threatened breach by Licensee of any of its agreements or obligations hereunder, Licensor shall have the right of injunction and the right to invoke any remedy allowed at law or in equity or otherwise as if entry, summary proceedings or other remedies were not provided for herein.

(d) In the event of entry by Licensor, Licensor at its option may store at the cost of Licensee any personal property of Licensee or its servants, employees and agents then in the Premises or in the Building, but in such case Licensor shall not be obligated to store such property for more than two months and thereafter may dispose of such property in any way it sees fit, upon 10 days notice in writing to Licensee. If Licensor shall sell such personal property, it shall be entitled to retain from the proceeds thereof the expense of the sale and the cost of the storage.

(e) The filing of a voluntary petition in bankruptcy by Licensee before or after commencement of the Period, whether for the purpose of seeking a reorganization or otherwise, or the admission in writing by Licensee of its inability to pay its debts generally as they become due shall constitute a breach of this Agreement, and in either such event this Agreement shall forthwith terminate without notice, entry or any other action by Licensor. Notwithstanding any other provisions of this Agreement, Licensor shall forthwith upon such termination be entitled to recover as its stipulated damages for such breach an amount equal to the amount payable by Licensee to Licensor under this Agreement for the remainder of the Period, and in any such case Licensor may file and prove its claim for such damages against the estate of Licensee.

17. Remedies Cumulative, No Waiver. Reference in this Agreement to any particular remedy shall not preclude Licensor from any other remedy at law or in equity. Licensor's failure to seek redress for violation of, or to insist upon strict performance of, any covenant or condition of this Agreement shall not prevent a subsequent act which would have originally constituted a violation from having all the force and effect of an original violation. No provision of this Agreement shall be deemed to have been waived by Licensor unless specific waiver thereof by Licensor shall be in writing.

18. Additional Expenses. Any expense or damage which Licensor may incur or sustain by reason of Licensee's non-compliance with any of the provisions of this Agreement shall be due and payable by Licensee to Licensor pursuant to the provisions of paragraph 22 of these Standard Terms and Conditions.

19. Payment Restrictions. If any moneys become due under this Agreement from Licensor or the ticket seller currently in charge of Licensor's Box Office to Licensee or any assignee or licensee of Licensee, and payment or transfer thereof is, or appears to Licensor to be, subject to Federal or other governmental licensing, withholding or other restrictive regulations, neither Licensor nor said ticket seller shall be obligated to pay over or transfer said moneys unless and until Licensor shall have been satisfied by Licensee that Licensor or such ticket seller may lawfully pay over or transfer such moneys in compliance with such regulations, and any such payment or transfer of any such moneys shall be subject to withholding if required under any such regulations.

20. Ancillary Rights. Licensor reserves and retains and Licensee expressly waives and relinquishes and grants to Licensor all rights to make or license or permit others to make motion pictures, phonograph, tape or other records, and live and delayed radio and television broadcasts of (a) the Event and any part thereof and (b) the Premises and any decorations, furnishings or equipment placed or maintained therein by Licensee or otherwise. Licensee grants to Licensor and its licensee and designees the right to use and to authorize others to use the name or names of Licensee, the Event, the individual and group particpants, players and performers in and sponsors of the Event, and the names and likenesses of any there of for the purpose of advertising and publicizing, except by way of endorsement, any such motion picture, record or broadcast and the products and services of any advertisers sponsoring the same.

21. Reference to Licensor's Name and Building. Licensee shall not circulate or publish or cause to be circulated or published any advertisement, ticket, placard, or other written or printed matter, or any photograph, motion picture, television tape, recording or other similar matter, wherein Licensor's name or the Building is mentioned or referred to without the prior written consent of Licensor.

22. Box Office Receipts, Service Charges, etc. All ticket sales relating to Licensee's use of the Premises under this Agreement shall be made by Licensor's Box Office at a scale of prices approved by Licensor, and the Box Office receipts after taxes shall be held by Licensor and applied in payment of all sums of money which shall become due from Licensee to Licensor hereunder or by reason of Licensee's use of the Premises as provided herein, including all amounts which shall become due for payments payable to Licensee to Licensor hereunder and for personnel, services, materials and equipment furnished to Licensee by Licensor under this Agreement, any agreement supplementing this Agreement, Licensee's work orders and requests, or otherwise. Any surplus remaining shall first be applied by Licensor in satisfaction of any remaining obligation or liability of Licensee to Licensor under this Agreement or otherwise. The aforesaid applications shall be deemed to have been made as and when said amounts become due, irrespective of the date upon which such applications shall be made upon the books of Licensor. Within a reasonable time after the Period, Licensor shall furnish to Licensee a statement showing all Box Office receipts relating to Licensee's use of the Premises hereunder and application of the same, and Licensor shall pay to Licensee such moneys as shall be due to Licensee. Licensee agrees to examine such statement and to notify Licensor in writing of any error in the account or of any objection to any charge within 10 days after the delivery or mailing of such statement, and unless Licensee shall notify Licensor of such claimed error or objection within such 10 days, such statement shall be deemed to be a true and correct statement of the account between Licensor and Licensee. Licensee agrees to pay Licensor promptly any amounts shown to be due Licensor on such statement, and unless Licensee shall notify Licensor of such claimed error or objection within such 10 days, such statement shall be deemed to be a true and correct statement of the account between Licensor and Licensee. Licensee agrees to pay Licensor promptly any amounts shown to be due Licensor on such statement which are not paid by the application of Box Office receipts. Licensee shall issue no complimentary tickets for the Event without the prior written consent of Licensor.

23. No Refund. If Licensee shall for any reason fail to occupy or to use the Premises as provided in this Agreement, no refund shall be made of any amounts paid by Licensee to Licensor hereunder, and the aggregate amount payable by Licensee to Licensor hereunder, including any disbursements or expenses incurred by Licensor in connection herewith, shall be payable by Licensee to Licensor.

24. Subordination. The provisions of this Agreement and Licensee's rights to the use of the Premises hereunder are hereby made subject and subordinate to the terms and conditions of the lease under which Licensor is a tenant of the premises on which the Building is located. If Licensor's tenancy expires or is terminated, with or without fault on its part, or if Licensor's lessor prevents the performance of this Agreement, Licensor shall not be liable to Licensee in any way.

25. Not Partners or Joint Ventures. Nothing contained in this Agreement shall be deemed to constitute Licensor and Licensee partners or joint venturers with each other or with any other party.

26. Force Majeure. If the Event cannot take place, in whole or in part, because of an Act of God, national emergency, war, labor dispute or any other cause beyond the control of Licensor, Licensor shall have no obligation or liability to Licensee as a result thereof.

27. Laws of . This Agreement shall be construed in accordance with the laws of

28. Notices. A bill, statement, notice or communication which Licensor may desire or be required to give to Licensee, including any notice of termination or expiration, shall be deemed sufficiently given or rendered if in writing and delivered to Licensee personally or sent by mail addressed to Licensee at Licensee's address set forth in this Agreement. The time of rendition of such bill or statement and of the giving of such notice or communication shall be deemed to be the time when the same is delivered or mailed to Licensee.

29. Headings. The headings of the paragraphs of this Agreement are inserted for convenience only and shall not be deemed to constitute a part of this Agreement.

Appendix D
Sample *Amusement Business* Concert Information

BOXSCORE

Among the top concert grosses reported through June 6, 1978:

FOGHAT, RAINBOW, HOUNDS — **$95,200, 11,900**, $9 & $8, Tom Makoul, Allenton (Pa.) Fairgrounds, sellout, May 28.

FOGHAT, SWEET — **$94,722, 11,709** (12,500), $8.50-$6.50, Tony Ruffino-Larry Vaughn Prods./TM Concerts, Nassau Veterans Memorial Coliseum, Uniondale, N.Y., June 2.

TOM JONES — **$93,238, 8,075** (17,261), $12.50-$9.50, Brimstone Prods., Edmonton (Alta.) Coliseum, May 26.

JEFFERSON STARSHIP, BOB WELCH — **$80,308, 10,750** (17,500), $7.75 & $6.75, DiCesare-Engler Prods., Civic Arena, Pittsburgh, Pa., June 3.

KINKS, CHARLIE — **$67,900, 8,400**, $8.50 & $7.50, Don Law Co., Boston Music Hall, two sellouts, June 4.

NAZARETH, GUESS WHO — **$65,883, 9,542** (17,048), $7.50-$5.50, Concert Prods. Int'l/Donald K. Donald, Edmonton (Alta.) Coliseum, May 16.

FOREIGNER, HEAD EAST — **$57,115, 7,609**, (8,000), $8 & $7, Entam, Freedom Hall, Johnson City, Tenn., June 3.

AMERICA, KATE TAYLOR — **$53,667, 6,537** (6,982), $8.50, DiCesare-Engler Prods., Stanley Theater, Pittsburgh, Pa., two shows, June 4.

FOREIGNER, BOB WELCH — **$47,456, 6,467** (7,500), $8 & $7, Entam, Roanoke (Va.) Civic Center, June 4.

154

FOREIGNER, HEAD EAST — $44,263, 5,905 (7,000), $8 & $7, Entam, Knoxville (Tenn.) Coliseum, June 1.

FOREIGNER, BOB WELCH — $43,839, 5,610 (7,500), $8 & $7, Entam, Greensboro (N.C.) Coliseum, June 2.

WILLIE NELSON, EMMYLOU HARRIS, BILLY JOE SHAVER — $35,212, 5,288 (9,714), $7.50 & $6, Sound Seventy Prods., Nashville Municipal Auditorium, May 26.

DOLLY PARTON, ANDREW GOLD — $31,839, 4,936 (8,738), $7-$5, Sound Seventy Prods., Von Braun Civic Center, Huntsville, Ala., May 26.

CHARLIE DANIELS BAND, FANDANGO — $26,182, 3,880 (6,800), $7 & $6.50, Tony Ruffino-Larry Vaughn Prods./Northeast Concerts, Bangor (Maine) Municipal Auditorium, June 2.

BOB MARLEY & THE WAILERS, IMPERIALS — $24,877, 3,313 (3,491), $7.50, DiCesare-Engler Prods., Stanley Theater, Pittsburgh, Pa., June 2.

RAINBOW, URIAH HEEP, NO DICE — $24,716, 3,456, $7.50 & $6.50, Monarch Entertainment Bureau, Capitol Theater, Passaic, N.J., sellout, June 2.

DOLLY PARTON, ANDREW GOLD — $24,478, 4,085 (6,483), $6.50 & $5.50, Sound Seventy Prods., Montgomery (Ala.) Civic Center, May 23.

LITTLE FEAT, JOHN HALL — $23,873, 3,187 (4,000), $8 & $7.50, Sunshine Promotions/Jam Prods., Indiana Convention Center, Indianapolis, May 27.

R.E.O. SPEEDWAGON & RAINBOW — $23,724, 3,200, $7.50 & $7, Cedric Kushner Prods., Palace Theater, Albany, N.Y., sellout, June 3.

TOM PETTY & THE HEARTBREAKERS, DAVID JOHANNSEN — $21,817, 2,909, $7.50, Wolf & Rissmiller Concerts, Santa Monica (Calif.) Civic Auditorium, sellout, June 5.

GARLAND JEFFRIES, JACQUES BLAIS — $19,000, 2,732 (5,000), $7.50, Donald K. Donald, Forum Concert Bowl, Montreal, June 3.

R.E.O. SPEEDWAGON, CHEAP TRICK — $18.314, 2,668 (2,932), $7 & $6, Festival East/Harvey & Corky Prods., Century Theater, Buffalo, N.Y., June 2.

ALVIN LEE & 10 YEARS LATER, DUDEK, FINNEGAN & KRUEGER — $16,532, 2,589 (7,000), $6.50 & $5.50, Pace Concerts, Houston Coliseum, May 30.

LITTLE FEAT, JOHN HALL — $16,532, 2,418, $7 & $6, Mid-South Concerts, Jackson (Miss.) Auditorium, sellout, May 30.

BRUCE SPRINGSTEEN, THE E STREET BAND — $15,105, 2,056 (3,800), $7.50, Sunshine Promotions, Indiana Convention Center, Indianapolis, June 6.

ELVIS COSTELLO, MINK DeVILLE, NICK LOWE — $14,980, 2,322 (3,000), $6.50 & $5.50, Wolf & Rissmiller Concerts, San Diego Civic Theater, May 31.

RENAISSANCE, AL DiMELOA — $14,613, 2,010 (2,557), $7.50 & $6.50, Caravan Concerts, Phoenix (Ariz.) Symphony Hall, May 30.

STANLEY CLARKE, ONE TRUTH BAND & JOHN McLAUGHLIN — $14,006, 2,010 (2,088), $7.50 & $6.50, Caravan Concerts, Popejoy Hall, University of New Mexico, Albuquerque, May 21.

KINKS, CHARLIE — $12,923, 1,723 (3,491), $7.50, DiCesare-Engler Prods., Stanley Theater, Pittsburgh, June 1.

RENAISSANCE, AL DiMEOLA — $12,556, 1,695 (2,349), $7.50 & $6.50, Caravan Concerts, Tucson (Ariz.) Community Center Music Hall, May 29.

STANLEY CLARKE, ONE TRUTH BAND & JOHN McLAUGHLIN — $11,602, 1,556 (15,025), $7.50 & $6.50, Caravan Concerts, Gammage Auditorium, Arizona State University, Tempe, May 23.

ELVIS COSTELLO, MINK DeVILLE — $10,800, 1,800, $6 Wolf & Rissmiller Concerts, Milliken High School, Long Beach, Calif., sellout, June 1.

ELVIS COSTELLO, MINK DeVILLE — $10,800, 1,800, $6 Wolf & Rissmiller Concerts, Hollywood (Calif.) High School, sellout, June 4.

BUDGIE, JUDAS PRIEST — $10,638, 1,725 (3,000), $6 Tom Makoul, Rockne Hall, Allentown, Pa., May 15.

ELVIS COSTELLO & THE ATTRACTIONS, MINK DeVILLE, NICK LOWE — $7,566, 1,019 (2,557), $7.50 & $6.50, Caravan Concerts, Phoenix (Ariz.) Symphony Hall, May 29.

STAN KENTON, GROVER, MARGRET, & ZA ZU ZAZ — $6,435, 780 (1,300), $8.50 & $7.50, in-house promotion, Morris Stage, Morristown, N.J., June 1.

ELVIS COSTELLO & THE ATTRACTIONS, MINK DeVILLE, NICK LOWE — $6,032, 815 (2,349), $7.50 & $6.50, Caravan Concerts, Tucson (Ariz.) Community Center Music Hall, May 28.

Appendix E
Sample *Billboard* Top Box Office Chart

Rank	ARTIST—Promoter, Facility, Dates *DENOTES SELLOUT PERFORMANCES	Total Ticket Sales	Ticket Price Scale	Gross Receipts
	Stadiums & Festivals (More Than 20,000)			
1	**BEACH BOYS/STEVE MILLER/PABLO CRUISE/STANKY BROWN**—Monarch Entertainment/ Concerts West/Jerry Weintraub/ WNEW-FM— Meadowlands, East Rutherford, N.J., June 25	61,128	$10-$12.50	$709,637*
2	**GRATEFUL DEAD/SANTANA/OUT-LAWS/EDDIE MONEY**—Bill Graham/ Concerts West-Autzen Stadium, Eugene, Ore., June 25	48,713	$11-$12.50	$512,236
	Arenas (6,000 To 20,000)			
1	**BEACH BOYS**—Ruffino & Vaughn/Concerts West/Jerry Weintraub-War Mem., Rochester N.Y., June 21	11,000	$7.50-$8.50	$82,500*
2	**AMERICA/PURE PRAIRE LEAGUE**—Feyline Presents Inc., Redrocks, Denver, Colo., June 25	9,000	$7.50-$8.50	$75,171*

Rank ARTIST—Promoter, Facility, Dates	Total Ticket Sales	Ticket Price Scale	Gross Receipts
3 BOZ SCAGGS/LITTLE RIVER BAND— Feyline Presents Inc., Redrocks, Denver, Colo., June 21	9,000	$7.50-$8.50	$74,374*
4 O'JAYS/PEABO BRYSON/SUN—Dimentions Unlimited, Civic Center, Baltimore, Wash., June 24	8,704	$6.50-$8.50	$68,949
5 HEART/BOB WELCH—Louis Messina-Pace Concerts/Mike Clark-Friends Prod., Mun. Col. Lubbock, Tex., June 22	8,772	$6-$7	$58,904
6 ALICE COOPER/CLIMAX BLUES BAND—Celebration Prod., Civic Center, Baltimore, Wash., June 21	7,181	$6-$8	$52,665
7 BRUCE SPRINGSTEEN/KENNY RANKIN—Feyline Presents Inc., Redrocks, Denver, Colo., June 20	6,315	$7-$8	$49,824
8 HEART/BOB WELCH—Contemporary Prod., Barton Col., Little Rock, Ark., June 25	7,032	$6.50-$7.50	$47,628
9 REO SPEEDWAGON/RAINBOW/NANTUCKET—Contemporary Prod., Omni, Atlanta, Ga., June 24	6,722	$6.50-$7.50	$47,607
10 TED NUGENT/BLACK OAK—Festival East Inc., Mem. Aud., Buffalo, N.Y., June 23	6,100	$6-$8	$45,433
11 BOB SEGER & THE SILVER BULLET BAND/RARE EARTH/TOBY BEAU— Avalon Attractions, Selland Arena, Fresno, Calif., June 20	7,333	$6	$43,998*
12 HEART/BOB WELCH—Mike Clark-Friends Prod./Louis Messina-Pace Concerts, Civic Center Col., Amarillo, Tex., June 20	5,143	$6-$7	$33,501
13 HEART/BOB WELCH—Pace Concerts/ Friends Prod., Taylor County Col., Abilene, Tex., June 23	4,091	$6-$7	$26,370
14 DOLLY PARTON/EDDIE RABBITT— Contemporary Prod., Hammons Center, Springfield, Mass., June 22	3,518	$7	$23,583

Auditoriums (Under 6,000)

Rank ARTIST—Promoter, Facility, Dates	Total Ticket Sales	Ticket Price Scale	Gross Receipts
1 JIMMY BUFFETT/DANNY O'KEEFE— Avalon Attractions, County Bowl, Santa Barbara, Calif., June 24	2,932	$6.50-$8.50	$24,198
2 KINKS/CHARLIE—Bill Graham, Community Thea., Berkeley, Calif., June 21	3,591	$5.50-$7.50	$24,139*

Rank ARTIST—Promoter, Facility, Dates	Total Ticket Sales	Ticket Price Scale	Gross Receipts
3 BRUCE SPRINGSTEEN—John Bauer Concerts, Paramount Thea., Seattle, Wash., June 25	2,976	$7-$8	$22,677*
4 CRUSADERS/NORMAN CONNERS— DiCesare Engler Prod., Stanley Thea., Pittsburgh, Pa., June 23	2,630	$7.50-$8.50	$21,040
5 BRUCE SPRINGSTEEN—John Bauer Concerts, Paramount Thea., Portland, Ore., June 24	2,504	$7-$8	$19,627
6 JOHN PRINE/MAC MacANALLY—Mid-South Concerts, Civic Center, Birmingham, Ala., June 25	2,307	$7	$16,149
7 JOHN PRINE/MAC MacANALLY—Mid-South Concerts, Orpheum Thea., Memphis, Tenn., June 23	2,305	$6-$7	$15,327
8 BILLY COBHAM & JOHN McLAUGHLIN—New Audiences, Warner Thea., Washington, D.C., June 20	2,000	$7.50	$15,000*
9 BILLY COBHAM & JOHN McLAUGHLIN—Barnette Lipman, Morris Stage, Morristown, N.J., June 19	1,300	$8.95-$9.95	$12,720*
10 ROY BUCHANAN/JOHN McLAUGHLIN—Stucky Prod., Thea., Tampa, Fla., June 23 (2)	2,015	$6	$12,090

Appendix F
Sample Investor Agreement

Towne House Concerts, Ltd.
May 27, 1976

Dear   :

As you know, Towne House Concerts, Ltd., and Concerts East are promoting a concert at Shea Stadium, Queens, New York, on Friday, July 23, 1976, featuring "Jethro Tull," "Robin Trower," and possibly others (hereinafter referred to as the "Concert"). This letter, when signed by you and by us, will confirm our agreement regarding your financial participation in the promotion of the Concert. Although you are entering into this agreement as an individual, we agree that you may assign all of your rights and obligations hereunder to a corporation to be designated by you, in which you are a principal stockholder; and upon such assignment you are hereby released and discharged from any personal liability under this agreement.

In consideration for your participation, as set forth below, you agree to pay to and in the name of Towne House Concerts, Ltd., the amount of Forty Thousand Dollars ($40,000). Said amount shall be paid in the following manner:

a) $10,000 to be paid upon execution of this letter agreement, which amount shall be used by Towne House Concerts to pay its share of the deposit required by the City of New York for use of Shea Stadium for the Concert.

b) $20,000 on or before June 18, 1976, which amount shall be used as talent deposits to be submitted to the responsible theatrical agency or agencies with contracts providing for the services of "Jethro Tull," "Robin Trower," and others, if any (which contracts will provide as follows: (1) "Jethro Tull": $50,000 guarantee plus 60% of gross receipts after 20% above the breakeven; (2) "Robin Trower": $35,000 flat guarantee; (3) other talent: $1,000). In the event that any artist does not perform for the Concert and the deposit for that artist is returned, Towne House Concerts, Ltd., agrees to hold said amount in escrow for your benefit, and for no other use unless otherwise agreed upon by you and by us; and the same shall be returned to you upon demand. It is intended that the Concert shall feature both "Jethro Tull" and "Robin Trower" and that should *either* attraction not execute contracts on the above terms, then the $20,000 intended to be used as talent deposits in this paragraph (b) shall not be so employed and shall be returned to you, and you shall have no further obligations under this agreement.

c) $10,000 on or before July 9, 1976, to be used only for Concert purposes.

Your participation interest shall be Twenty-Five (25%) percent of the Net Profits of the Concert. "Net Profits" shall mean gross receipts from ticket sales, less the actual expenses incurred for the categories set forth in the attached Schedule of Operating Expenses. It is understood and agreed that the expenses shall not exceed $268,500 plus possible percentage payments to talent as set forth above, and to the facility and ticket distribution as set forth in the attached Schedule. In the event the actual expenses other than above mentioned possible percentage payments exceed $268,500, the amount of such excess shall not be deducted from gross receipts in computing and determining your share of Net Profits.

If gross receipts do not equal or exceed the cumulative amount of all expenses (calculated in the same manner as set forth in the paragraph immediately preceding) you agree to be responsible for the first Five Thousand Dollars ($5,000) of net loss attributable to Towne House Concerts' share of such loss, i.e., if total Concert loss is $10,000 the Towne House Concerts' share is $5,000, which amount you will absorb; and if Towne House Concerts' share of such loss exceeds $5,000 we shall bear the excess equally with you. In no event, however, shall your share of the net loss, if any, exceed Forty Thousand Dollars ($40,000).

We will submit to you copies of all executed documents related to the Concert within five (5) days after receipt by us.

We will provide you with a statement of box-office receipts together with a breakdown of expenses upon conclusion of the Concert. This statement shall serve as a preliminary Profit and Loss Statement. We will provide you with a final and complete Profit and Loss Statement, with copies of receipts and bills for all expenses, on or before July 27, 1976. If the preliminary Profit and Loss Statement indicates that gross receipts will exceed the cumulative amount of all expenses, Towne House Concerts will reimburse you for the full amount of your $40,000 participatory investment as follows:

a) upon conclusion of the Concert, up to the amount and to the extent that the Stadium Box Office is holding proceeds which may be payable to Towne House Concerts that evening,

b) the balance on or before July 27, 1976,

c) in any event, however, if a Net Profit is indicated as provided above, you shall be reimbursed for your Forty Thousand Dollar ($40,000) investment prior to Towne House Concerts being paid its share of Net Profits.

In the event that the final Profit and Loss Statement indicates a Net Profit from the Concert, we shall pay you your Twenty-Five (25%) percent share of Net Profits on or before July 27, 1976.

If this meets with your approval and understanding, please sign a copy of this letter where indicated below.

Sincerely yours,
TOWNE HOUSE CONCERTS, LTD.

By: _____

Howard Stein, Executive Producer

Agreed and Accepted:

_____

Appendix G
AFM Artist Engagement License

THIS CONTRACT for the personal services of musicians on the engagement described

below, made this_____day of_____, 19___, between the undersigned

Purchaser of Music (herein called "Employer") and _____ musicians. (This contract does not conclusively determine the person liable to report and pay employment taxes and similar employer levies under the rulings of the U.S. Internal Revenue Service and of some state agencies.)

The musicians are engaged severally on the terms and conditions on the face hereof. The leader represents that the musicians already designated have agreed to be bound by said terms and conditions. Each musician yet to be chosen, upon acceptance, shall be bound by said terms and conditions. Each musician may enforce this agreement. The musicians severally agree to render services under the undersigned leader.

1. Name and Address of Place of Engagement _____

   Print Name of Band or Group_____

2. Date(s), starting and finishing time of engagement_____

163

3. Type of Engagement (specify whether dance, stage show, banquet, etc.) _____

_____

4. Wage Agreed Upon $ _____

(Terms and Amount)

_____

This wage includes expenses agreed to be reimbursed by the Employer in accordance with the attached schedule, or a schedule to be furnished the Employer on or before the date of engagement.

5. Employer will make payments as follows: _____

(Specify when payments are to be

_____

made)

Upon request by the Federation or the local in whose jurisdiction the musicians shall perform hereunder, Employer either shall make advance payment hereunder or shall post an appropriate bond.

If the engagement is subject to contribution to the A.F.M. & E.P.W. Pension Welfare Fund, the leader will collect same from the Employer and pay it to the Fund; and the Employer and leader agree to be bound by the Trust Indenture dated October 2, 1959, as amended, relating to services rendered hereunder in the U.S., and by the Agreement and Declaration of Trust dated April 9, 1962, as amended, relating to services rendered hereunder in Canada.

6. The Employer shall at all times have complete supervision, direction and control over the services of musicians on this engagement and expressly reserves the right to control the manner, means and details of the performance of services by the musicians including the leader as well as the ends to be accomplished. If any musicians have not been chosen upon the signing of this contract, the leader shall, as agent for the Employer and under his instructions, hire such persons and any replacements as are required.

7. In accordance with the Constitution, By-laws, Rules and Regulations of the Federation, the parties will submit every claim, dispute, controversy or difference involving the musical services arising out of or connected with this contract and the engagement covered thereby for determination by the International Executive Board of the Federation or a similar board of an appropriate local thereof and such determination shall be conclusive, final and binding upon the parties.

ADDITIONAL TERMS AND CONDITIONS:

The leader shall, as agent of the Employer, enforce disciplinary measures for just cause, and carry out instructions as to selections and manner of performance. The agreement of the musicians to perform is subject to proven detention by sickness, accidents, riots, strikes, epidemics, acts of God, or any other legitimate conditons beyond their control. On behalf of the Employer the leader will distribute the amount received from the Employer to the musicians, including himself as indicated on the opposite side of this contract, or in place thereof on separate memorandum supplied to the Employer at or before the commencement of the employment hereunder and take and turn over to the Employer receipts therefor from each musician, including himself. The amount paid to the leader includes the cost of transportation, which will be reported by the leader to the Employer.

All employees covered by the agreement must be members in good standing of the Federation. However, if the employment provided for hereunder is subject to the Labor-Management Relations Act, 1947, all employees who are members of the Federation when their employment commences hereunder shall be continued in such employment only so long as they continue such membership in good standing. All other employees covered by this agreement, on or before the thirtieth day following the commencement of their employment, or the effective date of this agreement, whichever is later, shall become and continue to be members in good standing of the Federation. The provisions of this paragraph shall not become effective unless and until permitted by applicable law.

To the extent permitted by applicable law, nothing in this contract shall ever be construed so as to interfere with any duty owing by any musician performing hereunder to the Federation pursuant to its Constitution, By-laws, Rules, Regulations and Orders.

Any musicians on this engagement are free to cease service hereunder by reason of any strike, ban, unfair list order or requirement of the Federation or of any Federation local approved by the Federation or by reason of any other labor dispute approved by the Federation, and shall be free to accept and engage in other employment of the same or similar character or otherwise, without any restraint, hindrance, penalty, obligation of similar character or otherwise, without any restraint, hindrance, penalty, obligation or liability whatever, any other provisions of this contract to the contrary notwithstanding.

Representatives of the Federation local in whose jurisdiction the musicians shall perform hereunder shall have access to the place of performance (except to private residences) for the purpose of conferring with the musicians.

No performance on the engagement shall be recorded, reproduced or transmitted from the place of performance, in any manner or by any means whatsoever, in the absence of a specific written agreement with the Federation relating to and permitting such recording, reproduction or transmission.

The Employer represents that there does not exist against him, in favor of any member of the Federation, any claim of any kind arising out of musical services rendered for such Employer. No musician will be required to perform any provisions of this contract or to render any services for said Employer as long as any such claim is unsatisfied or unpaid, in whole or in part. If the Employer breaches this agreement, he shall pay the musicians in addition to damages, 6% interest thereon plus a reasonable attorney's fee.

To the extent permitted by applicable law, all of the Constitution, By-Laws, Rules and Regulations of the Federation and of any local thereof applicable to this engagement (not in conflict with those of the Federation) will be adhered to and the parties acknowledge that they are and each has the obligation to be, fully acquainted therewith.

SPECIAL PROVISIONS:

Musicians' names or likenesses may not be used as an endorsement of any product or service nor in connection with any commercial tie-up without musicians' prior written consent.

Print Employer's Name		Print Leader's Name	Local No.
Signature of Employer		Signature of Leader	
Print Street Address		Print Street Address	
City State Zip Code		City State Zip Code	
Telephone			

Appendix H
AGVA Standard Form of Artists Engagement Contract

AGREEMENT made this _____ day of _____, 19____, between _____
_____
hereinafter called the "Operator Employer," whose address is _____
_____ and _____
hereinafter called the "Artist Employee," whose address is _____
_____ Social Security No. _____ (If AGVA Member,
give Membership No.) _____ AGVA Branch _____.

WHEREAS, the Operator Employer recognizes that the AMERICAN GUILD OF VARIETY ARTISTS (hereinafter called "AGVA") is the exclusive collective bargaining representative for all Artist Employees now or hereafter employed or engaged by the Operator Employer in the variety entertainment field, including the Artist Employee(s) engaged hereunder, and that AGVA has established the basic minimum terms and conditions of employment for said Artist Employee(s) in the variety entertainment field.

NOW, THEREFORE, in consideration of the foregoing, the execution of this Agreement by each of the parties hereto, and the full and faithful performance of the covenants, representations and warranties contained herein, it is agreed as follows:

1. The Operator Employee warrants that he is the Operator Employer herein at the present time and intends to be such for the duration of this contract, and engages the Artist Employee(s) and the Artist Employee(s) hereby accepts said en-

167

gagement, to present his/her act under the direction, supervision and control of the

Operator Employer as _____

_____consisting of _____ person(s), at the

| (Name of Establishment) | (Address of Establishment) |

in _____ in the city of _____
        (Room Artist Employee To Appear)

for·a period of _____ consecutive week(s) or _____ consecutive day(s), number of shows daily _____, and weekly _____ (exact number of shows weekly and daily must be specified) commencing on ____/____, 19__, for which the Operator Employer agrees to pay the Artist Employee(s) and the Artist Employee(s) agrees to accept, as full payment (all minimum scales are net, no commissions to be paid on minimum scales) the sum of $ dollars (weekly) or $ dollars (daily), payable immediately preceding the first performance on the concluding night of each week(s) or day(s) engagement hereunder, plus transportation. No transportation shall be paid by the Artist Employee(s).

2. OPTIONS AND NOTICE OF EXERCISE OF OPTIONS. The Artist Employee(s) hereby gives and grants to the Operator Employer the option of extending this agreement for _____ (   ) consecutive additional periods of _____ (   ) week(s) or _____ (   ) day(s) immediately following the conclusion of the original engagement hereunder, upon the same or better terms and conditions contained herein for the original period thereof. The weekly or daily compensation during each such option period provided herein shall be $_____ dollars ($) dollars. Each of these options to be effective must be exercised in writing by the Operator Employer no later than _____ (   ) week(s) or _____ (   ) day(s) prior to the termination of the Artist Employee(s) engagement. (NOTE: On engagements for one week or less AGVA Rules require written notice the day following the opening; on engagements of 2 or 3 weeks, the Rules require at least one week's written notice and on engagements of 4 or more weeks the Rules require at least 2 weeks' written notice prior to the termination of the Artist Employee(s) engagement. All copies of option notices shall be sent simultaneously to AGVA NATIONAL HEADQUARTERS by the Operator Employer.)

3. IN THE EVENT THE ENGAGEMENT OF THE ARTIST SHALL BE CONTINUED BY MUTUAL CONSENT BEYOND THE EXPIRATION DATE OF THIS CONTRACT (ORIGINAL TERM AND OPTION PERIOD, IF ANY) FOR A PERIOD OF ONE WEEK OR MORE, THE ARTIST EMPLOYEE(S) SHALL BE DEEMED TO BE ENGAGED BY THE OPERATOR EMPLOYER ON A CONTINUOUS EMPLOYMENT BASIS, SUBJECT TO ONE WEEK'S WRITTEN NOTICE OF TERMINATION BY EITHER PARTY TO THE OTHER. ALL OTHER PROVISIONS OF THE ORIGINAL CONTRACT SHALL CONTINUE IN FULL FORCE AND EFFECT THROUGHOUT SUCH CONTINUED ENGAGEMENT.

4. AGVA WELFARE TRUST FUND. The Operator Employer is advised of an AGVA Welfare Program, which provides for Welfare benefits for variety Artist Employee(s) within AGVA's jurisdiction, including Artist Employee(s) hereunder. To assure the benefits of said Welfare Program to said Artist Employee(s) engaged hereunder, the Operator Employer agrees to make contributions to the joint Union Management AGVA Welfare Trust Fund, according to the following schedule:

$1.50 per person per engagement per day (3 days is deemed a weekly payment).

$4.50 per person per week of six (6) consecutive days.

$5.00 per person per six (6) consecutive day week for engagement outside the Continental limits of the United States and Canada. The Operator Employer by making such contribution to the Trust, accepts and becomes a party to such Trust.

(A) CONTRIBUTION PROCEDURE:

(1) The Operator Employer shall issue a check in accordance with the above schedule consisting of an amount equal to coverage for the entire engagement of each Artist Employee(s) performing and employed in the Operator Employer's production and/or establishment.

(2) Checks for Welfare Trust Fund contributions must be made payable to the AGVA Welfare Trust Fund.

(3) Welfare Trust Fund Booking Reports listing the names of all Artist Employee(s) for whom such contributions are made must be attached to the check.

(4) IMPORTANT: Checks and Booking Reports must be mailed to the AGVA Welfare Trust Fund, 132 West 43 Street, New York, N.Y. 10036 prior to the first performance of the Artist Employee(s).

5. REHEARSALS: _____
                        (Place of Rehearsal)   (Time of Rehearsal)

The Operator Employer agrees that all rehearsals (if any) shall be subject to AGVA's Rules and Regulations.

6. FILING WITH AGVA. Two fully executed copies of this AGVA Artist Engagement Contract duly executed by all Artist Employee(s) employed hereunder, with all riders annexed thereto, shall be mailed by the Artist Employee(s) to the National Headquarters of AGVA, 1540 Broadway, New York, N.Y. 10036 and the AGVA Welfare Trust Fund Copy to 132 West 43rd Street, New York, N.Y. 10036 within forty-eight (48) hours after being executed and prior to the initial performance of the Artist Employee(s) covered hereunder.

7. The Artist Employee(s) shall render his act in the variety field exclusively to the Operator Employer throughout the actual period of services hereof unless otherwise provided herein or otherwise consented to by the Operator Employer in writing.

8. All the provisions of any Minimum Basic Agreement now existing or which may be entered into during the period of this contract between the Operator Employer and AGVA are incorporated herein, and made a part hereof, and shall govern the engagement of the Artist Employee(s) hereunder. However, nothing contained in said agreement shall prevent the Artist Employee(s) from negotiating

more favorable economic terms and conditions than are contained in said Minimum Basic Agreement.

9. The words "Artist Employee(s)" and "Operator Employer" as used herein include and apply to singular and plural members and all genders wheresoever the context hereof will so admit.

10. The Artist Employee(s) shall not be required to perform or appear nor shall the Operator Employer request or require the Artist Employee(s) to perform or appear, directly or indirectly, in television regardless of the point of origin of the telecast without first securing the written consent and approval thereto of AGVA.

11. The Operator Employer, throughout the term of this contract, at his own expense shall furnish to the Artist Employee(s) live musical accompaniment according to the usual standard of his establishment for all rehearsals and performances of the Artist Employee(s).

12. A copy of this contract must be filed with AGVA prior to the opening of engagement date stated above.

13. This contract is play or pay and shall not be cancelled.

14. The Operator Employer shall not request or require Artist Employee(s) to mix or solicit drinks from customers.

15. Artist Employee(s) name or likeness may not be used as an endorsement of any product or service nor in connection with any commercial tie-up, without Artist Employee(s) prior written consent.

16. ARBITRATION. All claims or disputes by either party (including AGVA) as to the application or interpretation of the terms and conditions of this agreement or the breach of any provisions thereof shall be attempted to be adjusted between the parties (including AGVA) and, in the event they are not satisfactorily resolved, they shall be submitted for arbitration to the Board of Mediation and Conciliation, if any, in the state in which the dispute arose, or if none, to the American Arbitration Association under its Rules then appertaining, by AGVA or the Operator Employer. The decision of the arbitrator shall be final and binding on all parties concerned. The cost of the arbitration and the compensation and expenses of the arbitrator shall be borne equally by the parties. Such arbitrations held before the American Arbitration Association shall be held in New York City whenever practical and whenever in the opinion of the AGVA Executive Board or the American Arbitration Association, the holding of such arbitration in New York City does not create substantial injustice to either party to the dispute. A claim, dispute or violation which has not been presented to AGVA, by certified mail, return receipt requested, within a period of thirty (30) days from the occurrence of the events giving rise thereto, or within only thirty (30) days after the termination of the engagement, shall be untimely and shall not be processed.

17. SECURITY. The Operator Employer shall deposit with AGVA NATIONAL HEADQUARTERS prior to the opening engagement of the Artist Employee(s) hereunder, security, in the form of cash, certified check or U.S. Treasury Bearer Bond, an amount equal to one week's total compensation, plus transportation for all Artist Employee(s) employed or engaged by the Operator Employer hereunder.

In the event the Operator Employer breaches or violates the above paragraph, AGVA in its discretion may withhold or cancel the performances of its Artist Employee(s) under this contract and shall further hold the Operator Employer responsible for all monies due the Artist Employee(s) under this Agreement.

All cash and/or certified checks so deposited with AGVA will be immediately placed by AGVA in an AGVA segregated special account. Interest, if any, on such salary security deposits shall be used for the administration of such accounts.

If U.S. Treasury Bearer Bond (must be full amount) the Operator Employer agrees to forward such Treasury Bearer Bond directly to the Irving Trust Company, ATT: Custody Department, 1290 Avenue of the Americas, New York, N.Y. 10019. The Operator Employee agrees to pay the service charge rendered by the Irving Trust Company for the servicing of the Operator Employer's Bond.

In the event of a default by the Operator Employer to pay the Artist Employee(s) compensation and transportation when due, provided the Artist Employee(s) has actually appeared and performed pursuant to this Agreement, or the Operator Employer issued a check in payment thereof which is not collectible, AGVA shall pay from security deposited by the Operator Employer, the compensation and transportation due the Artist Employee(s).

In the event of circumstances other than those in the above paragraph, the Operator Employer and AGVA agree all other disputes, claims, etc., will be submitted to arbitration in accord with Section 16 of this agreement and the decision of the arbitrator shall be final and binding on the parties concerned.

(A) The Operator Employer agrees to replenish the amount of salary security in the event of depletion of such security by reason of a default payment, or arbitrator award, within seven (7) days after written notice by AGVA to the Operator Employer.

(B) AGVA shall have thirty (30) days after receipt of the Operator Employer's written request for return of his salary security to authorize the return of such security.

18. GOVERNMENTAL BENEFITS. The Operator Employer agrees to abide by and live up to all present and future State, County, Municipal and Federal ordinances, rules, regulations, laws and statutes enacted for the protection of and more specifically applicable to employment of Artist Employee(s) hereunder. The Operator Employer assumes all responsibility for the payment of all applicable taxes and contributions under Workmen's Compensation, Unemployment Insurance, Social Security or any other law applicable thereto.

(A) RIDERS: Nothing contained herein shall prohibit any party hereto from annexing any riders to this Artists Engagement Contract to incorporate more favorable terms and conditions applicable to the specific employment or engagement contracted for, provided, however, that no such riders shall modify the printed provisions of this standard form and provided further that all riders must be initialed by the parties hereto and transmitted to AGVA pursuant to the provisions of Section 7. It is further understood that no rider or special provision annexed hereto, shall be binding upon the parties or have any legal force and effect if such rider or special provision is in conflict with any of the provisions of any Minimum Basic Agreement between AGVA and the Operator Employer and/or any provision of the Constitution, By-Laws, or Rules and Regulations of AGVA incorporated by reference herein.

19. The Operator Employer shall not request any Artist Employee(s) directly or indirectly to appear in or attend any benefit without first receiving written approval from Theatre Authority, Inc., 485 Fifth Avenue, New York, N.Y. 10017, and AGVA National Headquarters.

20. NO DISCRIMINATION. The Operator Employer shall not discriminate against any Artist Employee(s) because of his/her membership in AGVA, because of his/her filing of any claim or the processing of the same or because of any complaint he/she may make concerning the application of the provisions of this agreement, or a Minimum Basic Agreement, or because of his/her participation in lawful union business, nor shall any Artist Employee(s) be discriminated against because of his/her race, creed, religion, color or sex.

21. AGVA REPRESENTATION. The Operator Employer shall admit any authorized AGVA representative to visit the Artist Employee(s) or observe rehearsals or performances of the Operator Employer's production, or on other official business, at any reasonable time.

22. NO KICKBACKS. Neither the Operator Employer, nor its officers, agents, representatives or employees, shall solicit or receive from any Artist Employee(s) or other person representing an Artist Employee(s), shall offer or give to the Operator Employer, or its officers, agents, representatives or employees, or to any other person, a kickback. It shall be deemed a kickback to solicit or receive or to give or offer to give, directly or indirectly, any money, gift, gratuity or other thing of value, as an inducement to securing or maintaining an engagement; provided, however, that this Section shall not prohibit commissions paid by an Artist Employee(s) to an AGVA franchised agent.

23. The Operator Employer shall not request nor shall an Artist Employee(s) execute or deliver any release whereby any provisions of this agreement are waived or released without the prior written consent of AGVA NATIONAL HEADQUARTERS.

24. No Artist Employee(s) employed or engaged to perform services at the Operator Employer's establishment shall be required to cross a picket line established by a labor organization at the Operator Employer's premises and which picket line is approved by AGVA, nor shall any Artist Employee(s) be disciplined, or this agreement be considered/or deemed breached by the Artist Employee(s), by reason of such Artist Employee(s) refusal to cross such picket line.

25. BINDING EFFECT OF AGREEMENT. In the event the Operator Employer sells, transfers or assigns his business prior to the termination of this agreement, this agreement shall be applicable and binding upon the Operator Employer's transferees, successors and assigns and both the Operator Employer and any transferees, successors and assigns guarantee the complete performance of this contract for the full term thereof.

26. UNION RIGHTS. AGVA, by reason of the provisions of this Agreement, shall, in addition to the rights of the Artist Employee(s) provided hereunder, have the right to administer and enforce the provisions of this agreement.

27. UNION SECURITY. Subject to the provisions of the Labor Management Relations Act of 1947, as amended, it shall be a condition of employment hereunder that all Artist Employees covered by this agreement who are members of

AGVA in good standing on the date of execution of this agreement shall remain members in good standing throughout their employment and/or engagement with the Operator Employer, and those who are not members of AGVA on the date of execution of this agreement, shall, on the 30th day following execution of this agreement, become and remain members in good standing of AGVA. It shall also be a condition of employment that all Artist Employees covered by this agreement, shall, on or after the 30th day following the Artist Employee(s) first employment or engagement by the Operator Employer as a performer in the variety field of the entertainment industry, become and remain members of AGVA in good standing.

(A) The Operator Employer agrees to report to the AGVA National Office, Membership Department, within five (5) days of the first employment of a non-member of AGVA, giving the non-member's name, Social Security number, and first date of employment.

(B) Notwithstanding anything to the contrary herein, this paragraph shall not be applicable if all or any part thereof shall be in conflict with applicable law; provided, however, that if all or any part of this paragraph becomes permissable by virtue of a change in applicable law, whether by legislative or judicial action, the provisions of this paragraph held valid shall immediately apply.

28. SEVERABILITY. If any portion of this contract is in conflict with any applicable Federal or State Law now in force or hereafter enacted, such provision shall become inoperative, but all other provisions of this contract shall remain in full force and effect.

29. INTERPRETATION. This agreement shall be interpreted, construed and applied according to the laws of the State of New York and any action against the American Guild of Variety Artists shall be brought only in courts located in the County and State of New York.

IN WITNESS WHEREOF, the parties hereto have executed this contract on the date and year first above written.

OPERATOR EMPLOYER: _____
                    (Full name of Operator Employer, person, firm or corp.)

BY _____
              (Officer of corporation, partner or owner)

ARTIST EMPLOYEE

_____ and_____
    (Stage Name)   (Legal Name)

OTHER ARTIST EMPLOYEES IN ACT
(must be executed by the individual Artist Employees)

_____   _____

_____   _____

_____   _____

_____   _____

AGENT: The undersigned Agent certifies that he has obtained this engagement.

_____   _____
(Name of Agent)   (Association, if any)

Appendix I
Artist Concert Rider

RIDER TO CONTRACT DATED _____ BY AND BETWEEN _____

_____HEREINAFTER CALLED "THE PROMOTER" AND

_____HEREINAFTER CALLED "THE ACT."

   1. A deposit of 50% is payable by certified check or accepted bank draft or cash to _____on the signing of the contract.

   2. The contract is subject to immigration and naturalization clearance.

   3. Reference to the Act shall be deemed to refer to the Act as presently constituted.

   4. All four (4) present members of the Act will perform the engagement. If the Act desires, a fifth member may be added to the group. In the event of illness or incapacity of any member of the group they shall not be required to perform the engagement, in which case any monies heretofore paid by the Promoter for engagement shall be returned to the Promoter and neither party hereto nor the Act shall be under further obligation to each other regarding the engagement. It is agreed the Act will supply the Promoter with a Doctor's certificate in the event of illness or incapacity of any member of the group.

   5. The Act shall have 100% top billing and shall also have the full right of approval of all supporting acts together with the right to determine the length and nature of their performance(s) and placement in the show.

6. At any large open-air festival where the Act may not have top billing, the Act has 100% star billing and full rights of approval of order of billing. The Promoter shall provide a running order of performance, including times of appearances, of which the Act has full rights of approval. The Promoter agrees that the position of the Act in the running order is an integral part of the festival, although should the performance not run to schedule, the Act may elect to appear at its appointed time rather than in its position in the running order.

7. The Act shall receive 100% sole star billing in all advertising and publicity including but not limited to programmes, fliers, signs, lobby boards, marquees, newspapers and radio.

8. Where the Act is to perform a concert or show on which other acts are to perform, unless it is specifically agreed otherwise in the contract for a different arrangement, the Act is to close the show.

9. The Promoter is to provide the Act with a full proposed programme for the performance of which the Act has full rights of approval. It is understood that the adherence to the agreed programme is an integral part of the contract, and that the Act may at any stage insist that the Promoter takes such action as to ensure the agreed commencement of the performance of the Act without varying the running order of the show or varying the agreed playing time of the Act.

10. Unless otherwise stated, the Promoter is to provide for a performance of a minimum length of sixty (60) minutes and a maximum of ninety (90) minutes. The exact time, under any circumstances, will be at the sole discretion of the Act. It is understood and agreed that the Act's performance will not be interrupted by local curfew or building policies.

11. (a) The balance of the guaranteed sum and the percentage payment provided for on the face page of the contract shall be made in cash or certified check to _____ and paid directly to the Act's representative prior to the commencement of the Performance of the Act.

(b) There shall be a maximum of twenty-five (25) complimentary tickets that the Promoter shall distribute to accredited radio, television and newspaper personnel. The Promoter shall also supply the Act's representative up to a maximum of twenty-five (25) complimentary tickets, if requested, for the Act's guests.

(c) A representative of the Act shall have the right to be present in the box office on the date of the performance.

(d) The Promoter shall retain all ticket stubs and unsold tickets for a period of sixty (60) days and a representative of the Act shall have the full right to count and examine same.

(e) The percentage payment shall be accompanied by a written box office statement of this computation thereof, signed by the Employer, together with the ticket manifest as supplied by the ticket printer.

(f) A representative of the Act shall have the right to inspect the Promoter's books and records as related to the engagement, to verify the completeness and accuracy of the percentage payment.

12. No ticket shall have more than one admission price and that price shall be printed on the ticket and shown on the printer's ticket manifest. All tickets must be regular hard tickets or Ticketron tickets and not roll tickets. The Act has final approval of all ticket and box office procedures.

13. The Promoter agrees that he will not commit the Act as a group or any one of them to any personal appearances, interviews, or any other type of promotion or appearance without the prior consent of the Act.

14. The Promoter shall, at his expense, provide the Act with adequate private bathroom and dressing room facilities; all dressing rooms to be maintained at a comfortable temperature and the auditorium, particularly the stage area, to be properly air-conditioned. The Promoter shall also provide in the dressing room of the Act fresh fruits, cheeses, potato chips, 4 cases of beer, 1 case of Seven-Up and Coca Cola, 2 gallons of milk, 2 gallons of orange juice (natural), 1 gallon of apple juice, 6 gallons of spring water, 100 large Dixie cups, large quantity of ice and tea-making facilities (hot water, tea-bags, sugar and honey). In the event of the Act requiring hot food (i.e., fried chicken, pizzas, hamburgers and such like) on the night Promoter is to arrange for one of his employees to collect and deliver same to the dressing room. The dressing room facilities are to include one room for the Act, a room with appropriate electrical outlet for tuning-up and a room for the road crew. Dressing rooms must be accessible to stage without passing through audience area. However, if a situation should arise where the Act has to pass through the audience, eight (8) security guards must be present to escort the Act to and from the stage.

15. The Promoter shall provide two (2) chauffeur driven limousines to meet and transport the members of the Act from and to the airport, hotel and place of performance on the day of their arrival and the day of their departure. It is understood and agreed that the limousines shall be solely for transportation directly connected with this contract during the period of the engagement. The Promoter shall also provide a station wagon or small truck to transport personal baggage from and to the airport and hotel.

16. The Promoter shall, at his expense, employ an adequate number of security guards who shall protect the Act, their instruments and personal property prior to, during and after their performance. One security guard is to be stationed outside the dressing room area at all times from the arrival until the departure of the Act from the premises. All security arrangements shall be subject to the approval of the Act's road manager.

17. The Promoter must have the name and telephone number of a Doctor, who can be available at short notice should any member of the Act require medical attention.

18. There shall be no signs, placards, banners or other advertising material on or near the stage during the entire performance nor shall the Act's appearance be sponsored or in any manner tied in with any commercial product or company.

19. No part of the Act's performance, sound and sight may be broadcast, taped, filmed or otherwise recorded. In the event that the Promoter, his agents, servants, employees, contractors, etc. reproduce or cause to be reproduced the Act's performance in the form of film, tapes, or any other means of audio or visual reproductions, the Promoter shall pay to the Act the sum of twenty-five thousand ($25,000) dollars as liquidated damages in addition to all other legal remedies which the Act may have.

20. The Promoter agrees that he will not sell any products identified with the Act, or the individual members therein, at the place of performance or any adja-

cent place under his control, nor will he license third parties to do so or permit such sale by any third parties.

21. The Act shall have the sole right to sell souvenirs, programs, photographs and any other products identified with the Act on the premises of the place of performance without any participation in the proceeds with any other party with the exception of any concessionaire requirements.

22. The Act shall have the first choice in placing their instruments and public address system on the stage, and once so placed they shall not be moved. During the performance of the Act all musical equipment other than their own shall be well positioned behind theirs or in an area completely offstage.

23. The Promoter will provide the Act with a sound and light system from Showco Inc. for a fee of $3,000 (three thousand dollars) to be paid by the Promoter to the Act's representative. Such systems will be as specified by the Act to Showco Inc. who will supply a technical rider in addition to this one.

24. The Promoter shall provide and pay for hot food/box lunches, a case of beer, 2 gallons of milk and a supply of sodas for the Act's crew in the early afternoon, as they will not have the opportunity to go out to eat because of the work schedule.

25. The Promoter or a representative shall be available at the place of engagement on the day of performance for the entire day, from 12:00 noon, in case of last-minute requirements or queries.

26. In the event of a performance that is to be held outdoors, the Promoter must provide a suitable roof and cover in case of inclement weather. Provision is to be made for the proper grounding of the instruments so as not to constitute a danger or hazard to the group members. If the Promoter shall, because of inclement weather, determine not to present the show or concert, the Act shall, nevertheless, be paid in full contract price provided for in this contract, it being specifically understood and agreed that the Promoter's obligations hereunder to pay the Act shall not be modified, affected, curtailed or diminished because of rain or other adverse weather conditions. If a rain date has not been negotiated for, or is not possible, the Promoter confirms payment in full to the Act if scheduled performance is prevented or curtailed due to inclement weather.

27. The Act shall have the right to cancel this contract without liability if, in their sole and absolute judgment, riots or civil disorder might endanger the life or safety of the Act if the engagement is undertaken.

28. All of the provisions of the contract and rider are of the essence and the failure of the Promoter to comply with any of them shall constitute a breach.

ACCEPTED AND AGREED

BY: _____
                                    (Promoter)

BY: _____
                                    (Artist)

Appendix J
DBA Certificate for In-house Agency

201B—Certificate of Conducting
Business under an Assumed Name
for Individual

Julius Blumberg, Inc. Law Blank
Publishers, 80 Exchange Place at
Broadway, New York

BUSINESS CERTIFICATE

I HEREBY CERTIFY that I am conducting or transacting business under the name or designation of

HOWARD STEIN MEDIA

at

c/o Xenon
124 West 43rd Street

City or Town or   County of   State of New York.
     New York   New York

I FURTHER CERTIFY that I am the successor in interest to the person or persons heretofore using such name or names to carry on or conduct or transact business.

IN WITNESS WHEREOF, I have this   day of   19 ,
made and signed this certificate.

_____

179

*Print or type name.
*If under 21 years of age, state "I am _____ years of age".

STATE OF NEW YORK
COUNTY OF
ss.:

On this   day of   19   , before me personally appeared

Howard Stein

to me known and known to me to be the individual described in and who executed the foregoing certificate, and he thereupon duly acknowledged to me that he executed the same.

[NOTARY PUBLIC]

Glossary

Actual—the actual price of individual concert production materials contained on the PCA form

Administrative fee—a nonreturnable management fee covering the promoter's time and expense for concerts involving outside investors

Advanced—the deposit, or advanced money, needed to secure production materials contained in the PCA form

Advertising—newspaper ads, posters, stickers, radio commercials, TV commercials, and special gimmicks, such as skywriting, used to inform the public of future concerts

Aftertax income—the point immediately after break-even when the promoter begins sharing in the profits of a concert

Angel—wealthy individuals who invest in Broadway theater productions and rock shows

Backdrop—a large curtain, used at the rear of the stage, that prevents audience members from seeing the bare walls of the facility

Backup services—substitute stagehands, electricians, security

181

personnel, caterers, and other suppliers of production materials, to be listed on the promoter's telephone contact sheet as a production insurance cushion

Bonus—additional money earned by an attraction or production person for exceptional performance during the concert

Bonus spots—free radio or TV commercials used as an inducement by sales people to get business for their station

Booking agent—the exclusive employment advisor to the artist, responsible for bringing the artist to the marketplace and for negotiating artist fees with concert promoters, TV and motion picture producers, publishers, and other talent buyers

Break-even—a figure whose sum reflects the total cost of a concert production, including the artist's guarantee, facility rent, rider demands, production personnel, and taxes; after this point, percentage computations involving the artist and promoter begin

Budget—PCA form column used for estimating the cost of various production materials

Cables—electrical cords used to connect sound and lighting equipment to the facility's power outlets; not to be overlooked when computing total production costs

Camera ready artwork—finished newspaper advertisements, mounted on heavy cardboard, ready to go to the printer

Cartage—the cost of garbage collection and removal

Club—the smallest concert venue, used primarily in rock music for exposure and seasoning of start-up attractions

Club date—the booking of an attraction at a club

Company manager—a production assistant and labor negotiator in the Broadway theatrical business

Complimentary tickets—free tickets furnished by the promoter to the attraction, facility, business associates, and friends

Concert hall—a medium-sized indoor facility whose seating capacity is somewhere between the club and sports arena

Concert promoter—a person who presents artists in concert and is responsible for every element of the production process, from negotiating talent to settling up in the box office

Concert rider—an addendum to standard face contracts that lists an attraction's production and living needs for a specific indoor or outdoor concert

Concessionaire—a person who sells programs, souvenirs, T-shirts, posters, or other merchandising products associated with rock music at the facility

Co-op advertising—any newspaper, radio, TV, or other form of advertising where costs are shared among the promoter, record company, or personal manager of the attraction

Deposit—an advanced payment required to secure the services of an attraction and facility for a future concert

Developmental role—a condition wherein the concert promoter can help the booking agency develop its new acts through club dates

Directors—head ushers

Downside—the promoter's loss potential

Exclusivity—a situation in which the concert promoter gains full or partial control of booking rock attractions at a facility, and prevents other promoters from using that venue without his involvement

External security—uniformed and plainclothes city police who patrol the outside of the facility before and during a concert

Facility manager—the person in charge of booking rock concerts at a hall or sports arena

Finished commercials—radio or TV spots that have been completely produced, and are ready to be played on the air without further editing

Firm acceptance—a confirmation by the promoter that he will present a show at the facility on one of several dates previously held by that facility

Firm offer—a notification, either by telephone or in writing, that the promoter desires to engage an attraction or facility on one of several possible dates

Flat fee—a monetary payment that does not involve overages or PCs

Force majeur—anything that prevents a concert from taking place due to forces beyond the control of a promoter, agent, manager, or attraction

Freebies—complimentary tickets

GP—abbreviation for gross potential

General manager—a production assistant and labor negotiator in the Broadway theatrical business

Graphics designer—a person employed by the concert promoter to prepare print ads

Gross potential—the amount of dollars that can be taken in if every available seat in the facility is sold

Guarantee—a nonreturnable flat fee, usually paid in installments, as compensation for the services of an attraction or facility

Hard tickets—regular printed tickets, dispensed one at a time (not a roll of tickets)

Headliner—the main attraction of a particular concert

Holding a date—the marking off, in a facility's master calendar, of all potential dates desired by a promoter, to be held without contest until either the promoter makes a firm acceptance, or the facility notifies the promoter that someone else has made a firm offer for the dates

Hostess—an employee of the promoter who supervises the catering of meals

House manager—an employee of the facility, responsible for everything that goes on inside the hall with the exception of the stage and backstage areas

In-house ad agency—the promoter's wholly owned advertising entity, whose existence can save him 15 percent off the normal price of buying newspaper, radio, and TV ads

Internal security—the facility's uniformed security and T-shirted security, used to patrol the inside of the venue

Janitor—the person who oversees the mechanical operations of the facility

License fee—a payment to the attraction's performing rights society (ASCAP, BMI, or SESAC) for permission to perform copyrighted music in a public forum where admission has been charged

Lighting truss—a large, rectangular maze of pipes to which the stage lights are connected

Local musicians—members of the local musicians union (not the act's side men) who may technically be "on call" during the performance, and therefore must receive minimum scale compensation

Maintenance—the upkeep of the facility (a PCA form entry)

Make-good commercials—free radio advertisements used to compensate the promoter for poorly read spots, or for spots that did not run according to schedule

Marquee—the large sign outside the facility used to announce upcoming events

Matron—a woman assigned to work in the Ladies' Room during a concert

Mechanical—a hard board on which the graphics designer will paste together a finished print ad for the promoter

Middle-level act—an attraction whose ranking is somewhere between start-up and major

Off-peak hours—advertising time during which the station's listenership is less than at other times

100 percent sole star billing—on a scale from 1 to 100 percent, no word or name can be larger than that of the headliner

On-air promotions—radio offers of free tickets, T-shirts, or record albums featuring the promoter's upcoming headliner attraction

Opening act—the attraction that starts the rock concert

Overage—any money that is left beyond break-even

Over-the-hill acts—attractions that at one time were authentic superstars, but can no longer command exorbitant fees (their rider demands, however, may still be excessive)

Overtime—time-and-a-half or double-time payments to production personnel whose work cannot be completed during normal employment hours

PC—abbreviation for percentage

PR—abbreviation for public relations

Packaging—the selection, usually by the headliner's booking agency, of the support attraction that will play with the headliner

Percentage payment—the condition in which an attraction or facility will receive a portion of either the GP or overage as full or partial payment for their services

Personal manager—a person who advises the artist how best to develop and package his talent

Porters—people who clean up the facility after a concert

Press kit—a packet of information concerning the attraction that includes a biography, photographs, and concert and record reviews, all arranged in a handsome folder

Prime time—peak listening hours on the radio station, with accompanying higher advertising rates than for off-peak hours

Production coordinator—a person employed by the promoter who coordinates various elements of the concert, and advises the promoter whether certain kinds of production work should be done

Production personnel—the labor force responsible for everything that happens onstage or behind stage, including stagehands, Teamsters, nonunion helpers, the attraction's road crew, and the promoter's production employees

Proscenium—the wall that frames a permanent stage in a concert hall

Public relations—newspaper, radio, and TV coverage of rock concerts in story or interview form, rather than paid advertising

Publicist—the person employed to do PR work

Replay dates—make-up dates for concerts that were canceled

Roadies—colloquial term for the road crew

Road crew—the attraction's traveling production team, in charge of transporting, setting up, and dismantling the act's equipment and stage props

Road manager—the person in charge of the road crew; also, the liaison between the attraction's personal manager and the concert promoter

Scaffolding—building materials used to construct portable stages, lighting towers, and other temporary concert edifices

Scaling the house—the selection by the promoter of ticket prices for each area of the facility—orchestra, boxes, loge, balconies—in order to compute the GP for a concert, and determine whether ticket prices are fair

Scalpers—people who buy up blocks of seats for a concert in hopes of selling them at inflated prices to people in desperate need of attending the show

Seating capacity—the maximum number of seats a facility holds, not accounting for seats that will be cordoned off for production purposes, or used for complimentary seating

Sellout—a condition where every available ticket in the facility has been sold

Seller's market—the true state of the concert promotion business, where the buyers (concert promoters) of talent are many, and the sellers (agents) of major headliners are few and enormously powerful

Shortfall insurance—a guarantee, usually by the attraction's record company, that the promoter will not lose money showcasing the act in his facility

Sound and lights—the sophisticated amplifying and lighting equipment used in rock performances, considered as important today as the music

Split-payment approach—the condition where a promoter will receive only a portion of his potential concert income immediately after break-even, thereby insuring that the promter will continue working toward a sellout

Stagehands—the men who physically put on a rock show

Stage manager—an employee of the promoter, whose job is to assist in any way the construction of the attraction's concert set

Start-up acts—attractions who have just inaugurated their careers

Stretch concert—a second performance, usually the day after a completely sold-out show featuring the same attraction

Strip ads—long single-column newspaper ads that command the reader's attention, yet enable the promoter to conserve advertising costs by announcing many upcoming events in one space

Sunday premiums—the added cost promoters are charged by various unions for staging concerts on Sunday

Superstars—the only attractions that insure concert promoters of guaranteed sellouts

Support attractions—the act that accompanies a headliner, but plays before it

Telephone contact sheet—the promoter's list of key production personnel and backup and emergency services, used on the day of the concert (if not sooner)

Telephone person—the facility employee who advises potential customers which seats are still available for a rock show

Ticketron—a computerized ticket service that enables customers to purchase tickets without going to the facility's box office

Ticket brokers—agents who distribute tickets as a service to the promoter, charging a small commission for every ticket sold through their branch offices

Ticket manifest—a form used to itemize where tickets have been sold (i.e., facility box office, Ticketron, agencies, mail order) and how many were sold

Ticket takers—the people who tear customers' tickets in half, return the stub to the customer, and save the rest for later accounting in the facility's box office

Times—a radio station's listing of when commercials are scheduled for broadcast

Track record—the number of concerts a promoter has produced, where, and how successful they were

Treasurer—facility employee in charge of selling tickets

Union Steward—facility employee in charge of the stage and backstage area

Unreserved seating—a condition whereby members of the audience can sit anywhere they wish in the facility, on a first come, first served basis

Up front—colloquial phrase for payment in advance

Upside—the promoter's profit potential

Ushers—people who seat the audience at a concert

Valets—men assigned to work in the Men's Room during a show

Variance—the difference between what the promoter budgeted for an item on the PCA form, and what it actually cost the promoter to obtain

Venue—synonym for a facility